Praise for Degrees of Deception

"In post-World War II America, many colleges, aided by the GI bill, nobly helped returning veterans obtain a quality education. It was our duty, done gladly, to help veterans who served heroically at Pearl Harbor, D-Day, The Bulge, and other battles in other wars. The educational system let them do this, and be honored in return. Today, many for-profit colleges manipulate that same system by demanding excessive profit at the expense of veterans and taxpayers. Kevin Connell, an excellent writer and future academic, focuses on how for-profit colleges mock the military's mantra of 'duty, honor, country'—and how America calls it the Nation's most highly-admired institution. This is a fine first book by a talented young author. Reading it will open your eyes—and make you guard your wallet."—Curt Smith, author of 16 books, including his newest, the best-selling *George H. W. Bush: Character at the Core*. He is a senior lecturer of English at the University of Rochester, a GateHouse Media columnist, and writer for such publications as *Newsweek*, *New York Times*, and *Washington Post*. Smith also is a former speechwriter for former president George H. W. Bush, writing more speeches for him than anyone in the Bush 41 White House.

"This is a MUST read. Meticulous and powerful research gives voice to the many student victims who are trapped by charlatans selling the American dream for profit. *Degrees of Deception* brings much needed light into this politically dark corner of private enterprise. It offers hope for justice and accountability to victims who suffered dreams broken by greed. An important rock thrown by a brave David at a Goliath of a deceptive industry."—Patricia O'Grady, Ph.D., former dean, Argosy University

"Provocative, bold, and innovative. Kevin Connell proposes serious reforms to what he believes to be one of the largest problems in higher education today: for-profit colleges and their public financing. In this book, Kevin Connell explains to readers that redirecting federal funds from wasteful for-profit colleges to affordable public higher education alternatives better serves the interests of students and taxpayers."—Anthony Y. Gu, professor of finance, State University of New York at Geneseo, Fulbright Scholar 2005–2006

"A compelling expose of the scandal masquerading as the for-profit education industry. Spanning this industry's inception and up to its current incarnation, Kevin Connell has named the guilty and exposed the techniques designed not just to fleece the general public, but also to cheat our military veterans of their hard won benefits and even their futures. If you have gone to school, are thinking of going to school, or pay U.S. taxes . . .

read *Degrees of Deception*."—Vince Martin, former admissions advisor, Everest University

"My story is not just one chapter in this book, but a collection of many. More than anything, I was affected by predatory lending at ITT after my admissions advisor signed my name to Navient student loans without my knowledge or permission. I am still fighting to have the loan taken off my credit, but neither ITT nor Navient will listen to me. *Degrees of Deception* gives me a voice to finally be heard. Read this book and avoid making the same mistake I did."—Vicki Plunkett, former student at ITT Technical Institute

"Kevin Connell's book, *Degrees of Deception*, is a chivalrous book—a zeitgeist. It maps my own victimization with eerie precision. I feel vindicated now that these colleges are finally getting their 'over' due. My recruiter shamelessly HOOK, LINE, and SINKERed me at a vulnerable time when I was a full-time caregiver for my dying husband who had been sick for 16 years with a devastating illness. This college struck and blindsided me, taking with them all our residual savings and secured two loans to ensure a future parasitic drain that can never be recouped."—Rose E. Grier, former student at Argosy University

"The concise workings of Kevin Connell and the description of the devastation for-profit colleges convey to students are heartbreakingly accurate. *Degrees of Deception* should be strongly suggested and distributed amongst individuals whom are looking to better their future through the education system. Kevin Connell wholeheartedly pin points the corruption in which I have first-handedly dealt with, and I am feeling forever grateful that I have crossed Kevin Connell's path. He has taken a strong role and advocacy of student rights. I wanted a diploma and a job and all I received was overconsumption of debt and disappointment. With this book, he can help people not become a statistic such as myself."— Sara Pierce, former student at Kaplan University

DEGREES OF DECEPTION

DEGREES OF DECEPTION

AMERICA'S FOR-PROFIT HIGHER EDUCATION FRAUD

Kevin Connell

ROWMAN & LITTLEFIELD
Lanham • Boulder • New York • London

Published by Rowman & Littlefield
A wholly owned subsidiary of The Rowman & Littlefield Publishing Group, Inc.
4501 Forbes Boulevard, Suite 200, Lanham, Maryland 20706
www.rowman.com

Unit A, Whitacre Mews, 26-34 Stannary Street, London SE11 4AB

British Library Cataloguing in Publication Information Available

Library of Congress Cataloging-in-Publication Data

Names: Connell, Kevin, 1992- author.
Title: Degrees of deception : America's for-profit higher education fraud / Kevin Connell.
Description: Lanham : Rowman & Littlefield, [2016] | Includes bibliographical references and index.
Identifiers: LCCN 2015043062| ISBN 9781475826050 (hardcover : alk. paper) | ISBN 9781475826067 (pbk. : alk. paper)
Subjects: LCSH: For-profit universities and colleges—Corrupt practices—United States.
Classification: LCC LB2328.52.U6 C66 2016 | DDC 378/.04—dc23
LC record available at http://lccn.loc.gov/2015043062

∞™ The paper used in this publication meets the minimum requirements of American National Standard for Information Sciences Permanence of Paper for Printed Library Materials, ANSI/NISO Z39.48-1992.

Printed in the United States of America

For Mom

CONTENTS

FOREWORD

Higher education has always been close to the core of America's vision of itself. As the distinguished educational historian Frederick Rudolph wrote in 1962,

> One unwritten law of the early history of education in the United States would be: Where there are no elementary or secondary schools, there you will find a college. . . .
>
> College-founding in the nineteenth century was undertaken in the same spirit as canal-building, cotton-ginning, farming, and gold-mining. . . . All were touched by the American faith in tomorrow, in the unquestionable capacity of Americans to achieve a better world. In the founding of colleges, reason could not combat the romantic belief in endless progress.[1]

That vision, and an eclectic mix of public and private institutions now numbering in the thousands, has produced a higher-educational system that, at least at its upper reaches, is considered unparalleled in the world.

Yet, while there is much to celebrate, it is also the case that this unquestioned faith in higher education inevitably results in American-sized excesses. While obtaining a college degree is almost certainly a good investment considered at the microlevel of an individual, problems arise when it is converted to a macrolevel (as it often, uncritically, is): that a college education is a worthwhile endeavor for *everyone*—almost at whatever cost. Moreover, this American faith in higher education is coupled with another uniquely American element: the ability of virtually anyone to start a "college" coupled with a political system that at times seems unwilling to limit what can be called a "college."

In this book, Kevin Connell examines with a critical eye the growth of for-profit institutions that have thrived in this American environment and that take advantage of an uncritical faith in higher education by individuals as well as government largess that lacks any critical focus. Spurred on by a profit motive, the resulting picture, unsurprisingly, isn't a pretty one. Indeed, as Kevin Connell lucidly examines, the overall picture is shockingly shabby: a system in which neither society nor the individual is remotely advantaged.

If the picture is of a diseased institution, then the remedial question of what to do about it is obvious but complex. In this book, having painted a picture of a for-profit system gone seriously amuck, Kevin Connell discusses solutions that are bold and sweeping. Ultimately, indeed, his conclusion is that "there is no other option than to eliminate them altogether." Recognizing that this option may, indeed, not be realized in the near future, this book, as Kevin Connell recognizes, advances the possibility that "there is something that each and every one of us can do to work toward progress on this issue," namely "educate the world around us of the injustice and corruption that exists in for-profit higher education." This book, in the best tradition of higher education, is ultimately about education. It is timely, sobering, and important for both individuals and society.

Thomas H. Jackson
Distinguished university professor and president emeritus
University of Rochester

ACKNOWLEDGMENTS

I consider this book to be many things. In its most literal form, this is an investigation of the greatest American con of our time: for-profit higher education. While the statistics surrounding the subject are shocking enough on their own, the real horror extends far beyond numbers on a spreadsheet, no matter how telling they might be. Among the millions of college students attempting to claw their ways out of debt, the victims of for-profit colleges have the greatest climb to make of any student in the United States. With each passing day, more and more people continue to fall unsuspectingly into the carefully placed trap of for-profit higher education. Once caught, these people have nowhere to go and no one to help. Ultimately, this book tells the story of the silently oppressed, and in sharing their message, I hope to give them back their voice. This call to action has been inspired by the people around me who have instilled and continue to instill in me a sense of empathy and courage to fight for those who cannot defend themselves.

This book owes a great deal to many people, first of whom is Ross Amstey. As my AP Language and Composition teacher at Rush-Henrietta High School, Mr. Amstey was the first educator to have a significant impact on my writing. Only after establishing a strong foundation of critical thinking and rhetorical writing skills under his care would I eventually have the capacity to write something of this scope. More importantly, Mr. Amstey instilled in me a love for the arts of writing and rhetoric, a gift that will remain with me for the rest of my life.

While I was writing this book as an undergraduate at the University of Rochester, several professors had a profound and lasting impact on me. Professors Gerald Gamm, Bill Tiberio, and Curt Smith are among the most influential instructors that I have learned from, both as a student and as a person. While they have provided me with a solid foundation of knowledge in a wide range of subjects, their greatest gift to me has been their service as personal role models of decency and compassion.

In regard to my research, the Senate Committee on Health, Education, Labor, and Pensions, under the leadership of Senator Tom Harkin, deserves an enormous amount of credit. Without the continual output of investigations and reports conducted by this committee and their staff, this book would not have been possible.

My family has also played an instrumental role in helping me through this grueling process. My aunt and uncle, Julianne and Paul Jordan, as well as my late grandmother, Marie Hanes, have all been a source of support for the growth and direction of the book. My Aunt Julianne in particular helped me throughout the final stages of the editing process, making the transition to publication possible. Finally, my grandfather, Leo Hanes, deserves special recognition in this regard. There were many times when I called him late at night for guidance and reassurance. Had he not been there to listen and offer words of encouragement, the writing process would have been nearly impossible to overcome.

Many friends have also gone to extraordinary efforts to help me through this process in a number of ways. Alex Yudelson, Zack Hilt, Adam Hotchkiss, Robert Marks, Greg Bischoping, Jared Jones, Brian Kos, Joseph Henderson, Tad Mack, Ben Stilson, Joe Morelle, Harry Bronson, Dan Gorman, Chris Fallon, Nannette Nocon, Evan Dawson, Cody Combs, Bob Newman, Bob and Colleen Regelsberger, Mark Lenzi, Paul McAndrews, Rafael E. Báez, Jake Sweely, Alexis Wallace, Jon Aho, Joseph Glick, and Myles Mack-Mercer were continuing sources of support and inspiration that helped see this project through to the end.

Finally, there are two individuals who stand out as deserving the highest praise of anyone for their efforts in the development of both this project and of me as a person. The first, and more directly associated with this book, is Professor Thomas H. Jackson, president emeritus of the University of Rochester. During most of my undergraduate education, I had the esteemed honor of working with Professor Jackson on this project in an independent study that spanned over the course of three years. This experience pushed the boundaries of my potential in ways that exceeded every other experience that I had at the University of Rochester. Not only has he been instrumental in offering valuable insight and assistance throughout this process, but he has also instilled in me the virtue of good character. Without his guidance and inspiration, not only would this book fail to exist, but I also would not be the person I am today.

The final person who deserves credit, who has influenced me more than any other in this world, is my mother. From the time I was a little boy, she attended every sporting event, concert, and award ceremony. If I had an event, she was there. If I was sick, she was there. If I needed a ride home from practice, she was there. If I was discouraged and needed someone to listen, she was there. She has always been there for me. Few sons are lucky enough to have had a mother who was as present and invested as my own. Her lifelong devotion to a career in primary education, steadfast determination to overcome adversity, and relentless love and support for me since the day I was born have all worked to collectively influence and sustain me more than any other person. Had it not been for her, I would not be equipped with the skills and character necessary to see this task through to the end. Inspired by her compassionate spirit and commitment to seeking justice, I gladly dedicate this book to her.

INTRODUCTION

THE WORST OF THE WORST

It is no secret that the pursuit of a higher education in America continues to become increasingly unaffordable in the early decades of the twenty-first century. Higher education, which was once the equivalent of workforce readiness for a reasonable cost, is now synonymous with dwindling job security and massive sums of debt.

College tuition and fees have surged by approximately 1,120 percent since records began in 1978—two times faster than health care and transportation costs, three times faster than housing prices, and four times faster than the increase in the hourly wage and consumer price index.[1] Consequently, the average household debt per student has increased dramatically over the course of this period.

As Pew Research Center reports, the average amount of money students borrow to attend college has increased from less than $10,000 in 1993 to more than $35,000 in 2015.[2] In total, student debt in America has accrued to more than $1.2 trillion, eclipsing credit card debt and standing now only second to mortgage debt.[3]

Although students enrolled in traditional, nonprofit higher-education institutions are met with serious challenges as a result of the circumstances, students who attend for-profit colleges face the most severe and concentrated harms of any student in America. Before venturing into the reasons this disparity between nonprofit and for-profit exists, it is crucial to first make clear the distinction between for-profit and nonprofit higher-education institutions.

The fundamental difference between the two types of higher education can be found in their structural management and primary missions. Contrary to their traditional, nonprofit competitors, which are run by independent boards of trustees, for-profit colleges are run by private corporations. As entities of larger holding companies chasing short-term returns, for-profit colleges are flawed in the sense that they use higher education as a means to maximize profit margins, regardless of the consequences that students face as a result.

It is not uncommon for large holding companies in America to operate businesses in a variety of markets, for example, a single holding company having interests in airlines, cellular phones, and so on. However, instead of a large corporation overseeing firms that handle airplanes and cell phones, these particular holding companies own smaller subsidiary firms that oversee the daily operations of for-profit colleges.

Because of specific institutional flaws found in a majority of these colleges, the quality and therefore the market value of degrees from for-profit colleges has been shown to be significantly lower than their nonprofit counterparts. According to the US Department of Education, while students at for-profit institutions only represent 12 percent of all higher-education enrollment, they hold 26 percent of all student loans and 47 percent of all student-loan dollars in default.

As a result of marketing practices, which I demonstrate are predatory in nature, students are herded into a system that will likely fail them. Of the minority of students who do graduate, an overwhelming majority find that their degrees from a for-profit college do little to obtain a job that gives them the capability to pay back their debts. This is the case due to a wide range of offenses including but not limited to predatory recruiting, insufficient student and career services, poor-quality programs, predatory lending and collection, manipulated job placement data, and strategic lobbying.

To prove the severity of the circumstances, this book exposes readers to the same journey that is taken by unsuspecting students who enroll each day in for-profit colleges. Following an opening chapter that describes the origin, evolution, and current dynamics of for-profit higher education, readers start out the same way prospective students do: with recruiting. From recruiting, readers are given additional insight into abuses committed against military service members, to which they are then exposed to the conditions as an enrolled student.

After highlighting inadequacies of the education that is provided, readers become familiar with predatory lending, manipulated job placement data, and the general conditions that follow a student's withdrawal or graduation from the college. From there, readers continue with a chapter on the strategic campaign contributions to members of Congress that insulate the status quo from reform, as well as a final chapter where readers are left with bold policy recommendations intended to advance comprehensive higher-education reform.

For-profit colleges undoubtedly pose the most concentrated threat to students in higher education, in that students who leave these institutions generally depart with significant amounts of debt and little to nothing to show for it. Therefore, it is the first purpose of this book to describe the current flaws of the for-profit college system and to establish a comprehensive plan to remove them from the national higher-educational system entirely.

I

THE FOR-PROFIT FRAMEWORK

The for-profit sector has been a part of the American education system for as long as there has been organized schooling in the United States.[1] Early examples, like the College at Henrico, "proposed in 1617 as part of a revenue-generating scheme for the cash-strapped Virginia Company," illustrate the historical bond between for-profit institutions and structured learning in America.[2]

Although fragments of a for-profit higher-education model existed in these early days of the colonial period, most American colleges of this era were the result of social and economic constructs that served two distinct interests.[3] These primary interests included religious institutions and land speculators. For religious institutions, colleges were "founded to advance the parochial cause of promoting a particular religious denomination rather than to promote higher learning."[4] Early universities, such as Harvard, Yale, and Dartmouth, were operated by Congregationalists to prepare men for ministerial and public service, and Anglicans established the College of William and Mary to prepare its clergymen for similar tasks.[5]

As for the interests of land speculators, "colleges were founded with an eye toward civic boosterism, intended to shore up a community's claim to be a major cultural and commercial center rather than a sleepy farm town."[6] Businesses would often gravitate toward these areas, which would "elevate the value of land in the town, and work to the benefit of major landholders."[7] Although speculators presumably encouraged enrollment for high levels of "civic boosterism," the boards in charge of operating these institutions were largely comprised of "local notables" who were influenced by the established clergy of the municipality.[8] These college executives often enforced strict admission requirements that served as barriers for most of the population, primarily as a mechanism to support existing class distinctions. For example, Harvard and Yale required all students to speak Latin verse and prose, while Princeton required all students to understand arithmetic in addition to Latin and Greek.[9] With the exception of a limited number of "practical" business schools, such as English grammar institutes appearing in New York City and Philadelphia by the mid-1700s, an overwhelming majority of Americans engaged in the historical trend of individual apprenticeship for training in any given trade.[10]

Although this education model persisted through the latter half of the 1700s, a new age of technological innovation quickly evolved by the end of the century, including Eli Whitney's cotton gin in 1794 and Robert Fulton's steam engine in 1807.[11] These innovations signaled an Industrial Revolution that would forever change the American job market. Demand for a larger and better-trained labor force presented an opportunity to for-profit schools hoping to expand with a curriculum focus on skill sets, allowing them to fill a niche that the parochial schools could not satisfy with traditional curriculum models of the time.

This "pioneer period," lasting from the 1820s to the 1850s, experienced the first significant establishment of large-scale for-profit colleges, such as the network of Bartlett schools that were founded by R. Montgomery Bartlett in Philadelphia, Pittsburgh, and Cincinnati between 1834 and 1838.[12] Marked by the "establishment of the early business colleges by individual entrepreneurs," this first era mastered the art of combining penmanship, arithmetic, and bookkeeping into one institution, establishing a "basic curriculum" upon which the new labor force was to be trained.[13]

With the decline of the pioneer period in the 1850s, there followed a "period of organization," which lasted from the 1850s to the 1890s. This era was marked by an aggressive and successful attempt by the for-profit industry to strategically mold its curriculum around "teaching students how to use new technologies such as the typewriter and telegraph," allowing the for-profits to hold a "virtual monopoly on business education."[14]

This for-profit campaign was led primarily by Henry B. Bryant and Henry D. Stratton, students at Folsom Business College in Cleveland. [15] Forming a partnership in 1853 with James W. Lusk, a professor of Spencerian penmanship in northern Ohio, they opened the Bryant and Stratton Mercantile College in Cleveland. Building upon their initial success, Bryant and Stratton branched out to several major cities in the Northeast and Midwest, including Buffalo in 1854, Chicago in 1866, and Albany in 1867. [16]

By the end of the decade, Bryant and Stratton had established colleges in forty-four locations, spanning from St. Louis to Boston. [17] This massive expansion by Bryant and Stratton was reflected in reports filed by the US Bureau of Education, which found that "from the estimated twenty [for-profit] colleges in operation in 1850, at least 250 institutions enrolling more than 81,000 students were operating in 1890." [18]

As the nineteenth century came to an end, the beginning of the twentieth century ushered in a third period, referred to as the "modern era." From its pinnacle role in the higher-education market in the late nineteenth century, the for-profit sector was soon "eclipsed by publicly supported institutions. Public secondary schools and large-grant colleges developed new models of vocational and practical education that undercut the market for the for-profit business colleges." [19]

Legislation, such as the Smith–Hughes Act in 1917, which firmly established the funding necessary for publicly supported vocational schools, worked to successfully confine the previously expanding for-profit market, sending the for-profits into decline. [20] Although the for-profits were able to survive due to the second wave of immigration to the United States from southern and eastern Europe, their sustainment was short lived with the economic trauma that ensued during the Great Depression. With the economy in shambles, few people had disposable income to attend college, causing many for-profit institutions to close their doors.

Facing the most desperate circumstances since its emergence in the early nineteenth century, the for-profit industry was on the brink of collapse. However, this all changed with a fundamental financial transformation that began with the GI bill, "which marked a switch in the relationship between the federal government and for-profit institutions." [21]

Because of the significant disadvantage that for-profits faced throughout the modern era relative to the government-subsidized public institutions, for-profits lobbied to be included at the table during the next round of government initiatives to promote postsecondary education throughout the 1940s and 1950s. Following this lobbying campaign, the for-profit industry was ultimately salvaged with its inclusion in federal funds under the GI bill in 1944, commencing the fourth historical period, the "federal student aid era."[22] Under the GI bill, for-profit institutions became eligible for federal postsecondary funds and participated in the educational benefits offered to veterans.

Attached to these funds were the eventual rules of accrediting requirements. These conditions were set to ensure that federal money would only go to programs that left students eligible to be employed in their respective fields by confirming that each program was accredited by occupational licensing boards before the funds were released.

With the creation of requirements for maintaining eligibility in 1952, subsequent federal programs shifted toward institutional accreditation. The National Association and Council of Business Schools created the Accrediting Commission for Business Schools to fulfill these requirements, and in 1956, the US Commission for Business Education officially acknowledged it. The National Defense Education Act of 1958 maintained this standard of institutional accreditation requirements and provided a policy foundation for the Higher Education Act of 1965. By the 1972 reauthorization of the Higher Education Act, the federal government solidified its extended financial commitment to the for-profit industry.

"By the end of the 1980's, the easy availability of student aid allowed for-profit schools to compete on equal footing with the lower-cost public sector, finally eliminating the price disadvantage that began nearly a hundred years earlier when subsidized business education began."[23] As the for-profit industry gained greater access to federal funds during this period, "scandals, fraud, and abuse dogged the sector, resulting in increasing regulation and external oversight of institutional activities."[24] From the evolving series of investigations conducted on the for-profit sector, the "reauthorization of the Higher Education Act in 1992 finally established rules directed at the specific abuses of the for-profit sector . . . establishing guidelines to rein in high-pressure recruitment practices traditionally employed in the sector."[25]

The wave of government oversight on the for-profit industry in the early 1990s coincided with the initiation of the current phase of the sector. Known as the "Wall Street era," this period is "marked by the new visibility of publicly owned corporate providers of higher education as the most prominent face of for-profit higher education."[26] Representing the beginning of this era was the "1994 initial public offering of the Apollo Group (owners of the University of Phoenix) . . . not because it was the first public corporation in the educational field, but because it epitomizes the new Wall Street focus on the sector."[27]

The consequence of this shift is primarily held in the expansion-centered education model that achieves economies of scale while ensuring that students remain eligible for federal aid, aside from the interests and outcomes of students.[28] However, this is not how the industry presents itself in advertising campaigns, which are notably focused entirely on the student. "Let's get to work," "Just make the call," "Find *Your* Voice!" Pulled as examples of television ads marketing for-profit colleges, these are the hopeful slogans being echoed over and over again to viewers, encouraging its target audience to believe that there are significant benefits to students who attend these institutions and that economies of scale are ultimately subordinate to these interests.

In addition to the prospective students who listen to these ads and believe that an education at a for-profit college is a sound investment, there are academics who are also confident in the for-profit sector amid otherwise uniform criticism of the industry. Kevin Kinser, professor of educational administration and policy studies at SUNY Albany and an expert on public policies and organizational structures related to the for-profit sector, has come to the defense of the widely criticized for-profit industry. He argues that, while "for-profit higher education is discussed as a single entity without recognizing the huge amount of institutional diversity in the sector," there is a rich variety of institutions throughout the industry.[29]

There have been several proposals to formally distinguish these different types of institutions, the first coming from the Accrediting Commission for Business Schools to distinguish colleges by "business" if they emphasize placement and training for employment, while others would be designated as "collegiate" if the emphasis was beyond purely vocational.[30] However, general education is becoming less and less a distinctive characteristic of these institutions.[31]

Then there is the proposal by Merisotis and Shedd that identifies two groups of for-profit institutions, which classifies career connector institutions and certificate institutions that are based on the proportion of awards the institution grants as certificates.[32] But Kinser argues that these two categories are "roughly equal" and "miss several important elements that are important in the for-profit sector today."[33]

Rejecting the simplicity of the earlier categorization proposals, Kinser ultimately endorses a scheme laid out by the Education Commission of the States (ECS): "Focusing on degree-granting institutions, the for-profit universe is divided into three categories: enterprise colleges, supersystems, and Internet institutions."[34] Enterprise colleges are "locally oriented institutions owned and managed by an individual, family or small corporation that generally have fewer than five hundred students enrolled in a single campus" and administer programs with a limited career-focused curriculum to meet regional needs.[35] Supersystems are described as "multistate, multi-campus institutions with stock that trades on Wall Street," notorious for "adding campuses in new regions and showing increased enrollment to meet the quarterly profit expectations of their shareholders."[36] The final category is Internet institutions, which "have no physical campus, deliver all of their programs over the Internet, and often have substantial international enrollments."[37] By dividing the for-profit industry into these separate categories, Kinser ultimately asserts that there is a biased focus on supersystems, which does not accurately reflect the collective makeup of the current sector.

Although this sounds like a reasonable claim, there are several key elements to the industry that disprove the notion that the for-profit sector has a rich diversity of significant institutions. According to investigations filed by the Senate Committee on Health, Education, Labor, and Pensions (HELP) in 2012, "at least 76 percent of students attending for-profit colleges were enrolled in a college owned by either a company traded on a major stock exchange or a college owned by a private equity firm."[38]

This means that, although the three distinctions made under the ECS model exist, more than three-quarters of the market consists of supersystems, while enterprises and Internet institutions only account for less than one-quarter of the remaining market share. While Kinser may be technically correct in asserting that there are hundreds of small enterprises in operation throughout the United States, this distorts the more relevant statistic in the proportion of students within each classification.

Additionally, the distinction between supersystems and Internet institutions is arguably misleading. The Senate HELP Committee found that each of the thirty major corporations investigated, otherwise classified as supersystems by the ECS, had either partially or entirely adopted Internet-serviced curriculum models. For example, Ashford University, owned and operated by Bridgepoint Education, Inc., enrolled more than "99 percent of its approximately 77,200 students exclusively online in 2010."[39] Under the Kinser-endorsed categorization rubric by the ECS, there are rigid distinctions between supersystems and Internet institutions. How can this be possible when Bridgepoint Education, Inc., as a publicly traded company on Wall Street, is also administering almost all of its programs online?

Although this in itself disproves Kinser's notion that the for-profit sector is significantly diverse, the growing bond between online programs and supersystems also illustrates a breakdown in Kinser's argument. Suzanne Mettler highlights that, not only have supersystems embraced online models, but also they have "led the way in offering online education—a move that other institutions are racing to catch up with and emulate."[40]

As I discuss in chapters 4 and 10, the decision to adopt online education has been derived entirely as way to fill seats and generate additional revenue from increased enrollment access and cheaper operating costs. With the adoption of online programs serving as an instrumental part of supersystem curriculum models, we can expect to see a growth in the market share of supersystems in the for-profit sector as a result of more accessible enrollment options for prospective students.

Conversely, there has not and will not be an adoption of online programs by enterprises because of the "locally oriented" nature of "institutions owned and managed by an individual, family or small corporation that generally have fewer than five hundred students enrolled in a single campus."[41] As Kinser affirms, "The growth of the for-profit sector . . . is closely paralleled with the development of online distance education."[42]

With supersystems investing heavily into online programs with massive amounts of capital and small mom-and-pop enterprises not having the resources nor the incentive to embrace the new wave of online curriculum, it is reasonable to suspect that supersystems will expand upon their already overwhelmingly large market share of 76 percent in the coming years. Consequently, there will be even less diversity in the future market compositions of the for-profit industry, further disproving Kinser's claim that there is too large of a focus on supersystems and not enough on the supposed rich diversity of the market as a whole.

The final two components of Kinser's defense of the for-profit sector coincide with one another. The first concerns the fact that the "for-profit sector has often provided a point of access for students who are underrepresented or denied participation in the traditional higher education sectors."[43] This is a point well taken. However, Kinser fails to recognize the unfortunate truth that *access* does not equate to *success*. Kinser's second component of this argument works to preemptively rebut an initial response by claiming that there is "little data available on student outcomes" and calling any findings that have been presented as being skewed because labor markets have "changed substantially" since these earlier investigations were conducted.[44] However, recent studies prove otherwise.

The findings of a two-year investigation concluded in 2012 by the Senate HELP Committee suggest that Professor Kinser is undoubtedly wrong in his assertion that the earlier studies are not reflective of the current reality. Under the direction of Committee Chair Tom Harkin, the Senate HELP Committee published a thorough report on the operation and status quo of the for-profit market. Its findings demonstrate that organizations making up an overwhelming percentage of the market deceitfully lure desperate people in the hundreds of thousands every year to sign on the dotted line, only to take advantage of them soon after.

In terms of student outcomes, withdrawal rates in the for-profit sector are staggering. These figures include averages of 62.9 percent of withdrawals from associate degree programs, 54.3 percent from bachelor degree programs, and 38.5 percent from certificate programs, which means that a final percentage of 54.4 percent of approximately 1.5 million students enrolled in the industry withdrew after an average median of 124 days.[45] In other terms, roughly 600,000 people in 2010 alone left without a degree roughly four months after the fact.

Compounding the misfortune of the hundreds of thousands of students who leave without a degree each year is the debt associated for leaving with nothing. Ninety-six percent of all enrollees in the for-profit sector borrow money through loans to pay for their education. Compared to this staggering figure, 13 percent of students at community colleges, 48 percent at four-year public colleges, and 57 percent at four-year private colleges borrow money in the form of college loans.[46]

In 2010, the for-profit industry held 1,559,091 students.[47] That means that, from this total figure, approximately 1,496,727 students invested in loans to pay for college. If the "easy availability of student aid allowing for-profit schools to compete on equal footing with the lower-cost public sector" has limited the "price disadvantage" of the pre–federal student aid era, then why are 96 percent of students at for-profit schools driven to take out loans, compared to their counterparts at community colleges and four-year public schools at 13 percent and 48 percent, respectively?

Due to high rates of withdrawal that parallel astronomically high borrowing rates with college loans, the end result for many is the inevitable outcome of default. Accounting for only 12 percent of total college enrollment nationwide, this small share of the market holds 26 percent of all college loans and 47 percent of all loan default.[48] Although Kinser claims that there are no reliable studies that are capable of predicting student outcomes and assumes that access is interchangeable with success, these figures portray a fundamentally different reality.

One of the most troubling components to this entire problem is the amount of federal funds that are appropriated to subsidize the for-profit sector each year. After accounting for federal aid through such programs as federal Stafford Loans and Pell Grants, 86 percent, or $32 billion of the for-profit industry, was financed with taxpayer money in 2010.[49] Even more startling is that, of the $32 billion, 19.7 percent of the total industry was recorded as net profit.[50] This means that roughly $6.3 billion of taxpayer money was transferred directly as profit to the holding companies overseeing the colleges nationwide.

Venturing into the even more bizarre, an average of 22.7 percent of the total revenue was spent on marketing and recruiting, while only 17.9 percent was spent on instruction.[51] How can we possibly spend more than $13 billion of taxpayer money on marketing and profit and only $5.7 billion on actual instruction and proceed to call that an appropriate federal investment that ensures student success?

With federal funds, for-profit colleges exercise aggressive marketing campaigns and predatory lending practices with the ultimate goal of maximizing profit. Here we find the fundamental flaw in financing and permitting for-profit education. In the for-profit industry, education is used as the means to maximize a profit margin at the expense of students and taxpayers alike. Starting at this baseline of understanding the nature of the for-profit sector, our analysis begins here.

ESSENTIAL TAKEAWAYS

The evolution of for-profit education has been both lengthy and profound. From its practical roots in the early nineteenth century under the pioneer period, for-profit colleges grew with the help of visionaries like Bryant and Stratton during the subsequent period of organization and eventually secured its long-term status by gaining access to federal funds during the modern era.

From there, the for-profit higher-education sector has exploded under the Wall Street era that still persists today. With the market dominated primarily by supersystem firms on Wall Street, for-profit colleges exploit students and taxpayers alike by funneling billions of dollars in federal higher-education funds into aggressive marketing and recruiting programs, while spending a proportionately insufficient amount of its resources on academics and career service programs.

As a consequence of the for-profit sector's devious development into a series of major corporations that place an emphasis on profit margins at the expense of its students, victims of the system find themselves in the most perilous position of any college student in America today. In order to fully grasp the weight of this crisis, the subsequent chapters of this book strategically guide our discussion through the same sequential process that the hundreds of thousands of students caught in this system endure on a daily basis.

2

HOOK, LINE, AND SINKER

Approaching the complexities of the for-profit industry, the most logical starting point for analysis should be where the average person unsuspectingly begins the costly entrance into the sector. Therefore, we open with the aggressive marketing and predatory recruiting scheme of the for-profit model. Documents show that in 2010, companies investigated from the for-profit sector employed approximately 35,202 recruiters, roughly 1 recruiter for every 44 students enrolled. [1]

Across the board, enrollment and revenue "quotas" stand as several "corporate objectives." These quotas are a predetermined number of students who are enrolled by the recruiter, otherwise known as "starts." "Total Enrollment Growth" of 9 percent, "Earnings Per Share" of 20 percent, and "Free Cash Flow" of 15 percent all stand as specific examples from an ITT[2] Performance Planning and Evaluation Form[3] completed in 2008. Similar objectives can be found at Corinthian Colleges, Inc.,[4] as managers closely monitored a series of "performance metrics for each recruiter, including appointments being set, interviews conducted, applications taken and daily enrollment."[5] To the even more extreme is an EDMC[6] corporate manager's e-mail from January 2008, which specifically outlined numerical objectives for several categories of recruiter business: "The goal is 100 March starts and we only have 47 on the books. So we must take no less than 15 March apps each week for the next 6 weeks."[7] Because of pressure being applied from upper-level management, recruiters have an incentive to use whatever means necessary to attain the highest number of "starts" as possible.

Due to high withdrawal rates, for reasons that I explain later in the book, high enrollment growth is vital to the success of the industry. As a result, deceptive and high-pressure sales tactics are employed to enroll large numbers of new students each year. The primary reason for all of this is to ensure investors that there will be enough students, or capital, to make a return on their investment. This practice is known as "churn."

A prime example of "churn in action," can be found in the case involving Corinthian, when it began the fiscal year of 2010 with 86,066 students and ended with 110,550. Over this time period, Corinthian experienced a gross growth of 24,484 students. However, during the same interval, 113,317 students left the company, either by graduation or withdrawal. Consequently, Corinthian had to enroll 135,034 students in the following year to sustain growth levels, demanded by investors as the threshold for investment.[8]

Another way for recruiters to satisfy the numbers demanded by corporate managers and investors is not only to increase enrollment but also the duration of that enrollment as well. As a result, there has been a massive push over the last two decades to grow associate's and bachelor's programs. This is done with the ultimate goal of transferring a majority of business from short-term certificate programs to two-year and four-year commitments for the students who avoid withdrawal.

"Until the 1990's, the sector was primarily composed of small trade schools that awarded certificates and diplomas in fields like air-conditioning repair, cosmetology, and truck driving. Two-thirds of for-profit colleges enrolled students in training programs lasting less than one year."[9] However, while certificate programs have grown over the past two decades, there has been an even sharper increase in the percentage of two-year and four-year degree programs. "Between 2004 and 2010, the amount of AA degrees awarded by for-profit colleges increased 77 percent and the amount of BA degrees awarded increased 136 percent."[10]

This emerging tactic, among others, such as expanding online programs, has proven to be particularly effective in the sale of institutional loans due to the prolonged period of financial commitment. As I further detail later, attached to these institutional loans are interest rates averaging between 13 and 18 percent, generating a significant amount of revenue as a result.[11]

With the motive of sustaining churn established, we can now examine how for-profit recruiters are able to secure high annual enrollment and promote extended academic programs. The immediate answer is that the success of this model hinges on predatory, high-pressure sales tactics. For starters, "Marketing and recruiting includes all spending on advertising, other marketing spending, lead generation, and the recruiting sales staff. Publicly traded for-profit education companies spent, on average, $248 million on marketing and recruiting in 2009."[12] So how is this 22.7 percent of the market share of marketing and recruiting spent? The answer to this question begins with the role of leads and lead generators.

Prior to any sales process, for-profit colleges conduct a massive contact information–gathering campaign targeted at prospective students. These "leads" are produced either directly by the for-profit colleges themselves or purchased from third-party firms known as "lead generators." Lead generators specialize in collecting contact information through a series of websites and then sell that information to for-profit entities for between $10 and $150 per lead, depending on the type and quality of the profile provided.[13]

This step in the aggressive process of netting hundreds of thousands of prospective students each year is vital to the operation of the for-profit industry. As one Kaplan, Inc.,[14] executive explains, "Everything on a campus or an Admissions department begins and ends with leads."[15] From the for-profit companies that have been examined, leads were purchased from at least sixty-two lead-generation firms, which were found to advertise themselves on "Web sites, billboards, and on TV as a free, safe, and reliable way to get information about college."[16] To no surprise, however, the only "free, safe, and reliable" information that was delivered to students was limited exclusively to the schools and programs that paid the lead generators.

The degree to which this "free, safe, and reliable" information is actually dependable and genuine has also been called into question. When a former lead generator employee was interviewed by the *Chronicle of Higher Education*, he revealed that "he told students that they would hear from their preferred public college, even though they almost never did. In the meantime, he said, they should consider attending a for-profit college—such as Kaplan University and Westwood College."[17]

In addition to the questionable process by which these transactions occur, relevant information is often altogether absent from these sites as well. Details ranging from tuition and fee information to curriculum choices are among much of the information that should be accessible to consumers but is frequently unavailable.

EarnMyDegree.com, for example, is a major lead generator that is guilty of such activity. "A search of the business administration degrees listed by the site only directs visitors to a page with a brief description of the demand and salary for business majors and invites users to request more information."[18] Moreover, when prospective students attempt to find information for "tuition" in the search engine, consumers are not only offered no specific information about tuition, but they also are rerouted to pages advertising how easily a degree can be attained and the potential pay grade in a related career field.[19]

Furthermore, aggressive television ads are also incorporated into the model to help drive prospective students to their websites. Education-Dynamics, for example, ran a commercial stressing online degrees. As "Make $25,000 more every year" flashes, a young woman sings the jingle, "If I earn a degree, I will make a bigger salary." It is worth noting that this all happens after the same woman emphasizes the flexibility of online programs and dances around in pajamas. Consumers, led under arguably false pretenses, are then directed to visit EducationConnection.com.[20] Like the other sixty or so lead generators examined, prospective students then fill out personal information forms on these sites to receive additional information.

Immediately after one of these forms is filled out, the lead generator then transfers that personal information to the for-profit college in exchange for a capital sum. These sums, as mentioned earlier, vary based on the material provided. This creates a mutual incentive to collect as much information as possible on those who visit the sites.

Once a series of transfers have been made, long lists of potential clients are then formulated and given to corporate executive managers to disperse to the lower recruiting staff. Soon after, the same people whose interests were originally piqued by an enticing television ad are then hit with a barrage of telephone calls from for-profit recruiters.

To find out firsthand exactly what this experience is like on behalf of those targeted, the "Government Accountability Office (GAO), as part of an undercover investigation, entered an investigator's name and number into a single lead generation site. Within 5 minutes, the GAO received the first calls from recruiters."[21] Over the course of the subsequent month, the investigator received more than 180 calls after logging only a single entry into one lead generation site.[22]

This example helps to illustrate exactly how aggressive this entire marketing scheme really is. Within one month's time following a single entry, the "consumer" received more than 180 calls, an average of 6 calls per day. Thinking in these terms makes it easier to now understand how and possibly why hundreds of thousands of people succumb to the pressure applied by the for-profit sector.

Once a prospective student is finally reached, recruiters are usually instructed to grill the lead with a series of questions, which tend to progressively escalate in intensity. This is intended to exploit points of emotional vulnerability, working to pressure thousands of prospective students to sign up immediately. As one ITT manager explained in a memo, "recruiters need to focus on . . . digging in and getting to the pain of each and every prospective student."[23] An ITT recruiter training presentation slide attempts to visualize what this process might look like, as a picture of a dentist pulling the tooth of a patient in agony is displayed under the title, "FIND OUT WHERE THEIR PAIN IS"[24] (see figure 2.1).

So how exactly are recruiters instructed to "find the pain"? We begin with the process of organizing the leads acquired by the lead genera-

Figure 2.1. **ITT Recruiter Training Slide. ITT, Increasing Your Scheduled to Conduct Ratio (ITT-00028362 at ITT-00028377). Retrieved from *For Profit Higher Education: The Failure to Safeguard the Federal Investment and Ensure Student Success*, 60.**

tors. After reviewing the circumstances surrounding each case, recruiters then know which questions will be the ones to have the greatest effect. For example, if there is a case that includes a young single mother struggling to support her four children, the questions will be tailored much differently than those to a middle-aged man with poor health who is struggling to pay his medical bills because he lacks health insurance.[25]

Once each case has been reviewed and the important details identified, recruiters then ask questions under the guidelines of a typical sales funnel. However, everything from the substance of the questions right down to the title of the funnel, found on an ITT internal memo to recruiters, makes these funnels not only atypical but troubling as well. Under the heading "Pain Funnel and Pain Puzzle" follows a four-tiered series of questions. As the supposed sales pitch draws on, the recruiter's script intensifies with the questions becoming "progressively more hurtful."[26] These tiers transition from the initial stage of "establishing rapport" to "digging for the motivation" to "feeling the pain" to finally "making the connection between the motivation and getting a degree"[27] (see figure 2.2).

Similar to ITT, Kaplan has implemented their own foundation of "ARTICHOKE," which deploys a similar method of "peeling back the layers" and "Getting to the PAIN."[28] In one message to recruiters, a Kaplan recruitment manager instructed,

> Keep digging until you uncover their pain, fears, and dreams. . . . If you get the prospect to think about how tough their situation is right now and if they discuss the life they can't give their family because they don't have a degree, you will dramatically increase your chances of gaining a commitment from the student! If you can stir up their emotions, you will create urgency![29]

So what kind of urgency is Kaplan talking about? Let us revisit the case of a single mother. Say a young woman in her early twenties is working three jobs in an attempt to support her four children. This "digging" might play out like the following script: Where do you live? Do you have children? Are you currently employed? What are the conditions of your employment? How much money do you make a month? After rent, utilities, and other bills, how much do you have left over from that initial sum? Does this limit ways you are able to provide for your family?

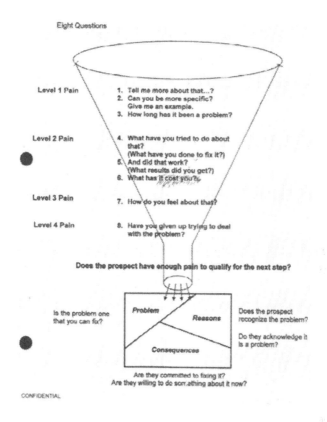

Eight Questions

Level 1 Pain

1. Tell me more about that...?
2. Can you be more specific?
   Give me an example.
3. How long has it been a problem?

Level 2 Pain

4. What have you tried to do about that?
   (What have you done to fix it?)
5. And did that work?
   (What results did you get?)
6. What has it cost you?

Level 3 Pain

7. How do you feel about that?

Level 4 Pain

8. Have you given up trying to deal with the problem?

Does the prospect have enough pain to qualify for the next step?

Is the problem one that you can fix?

Problem

Reasons

Consequences

Does the prospect recognize the problem?

Do they acknowledge it is a problem?

Are they committed to fixing it?
Are they willing to do something about it now?

CONFIDENTIAL

Figure 2.2. ITT, Completed Phoning Techniques Training Worksheet. ITT, Completed Phoning Techniques Training Worksheet (ITT-00015566). The company asserts that this document was created and used by only a few campus-level employees and never approved by the corporate office. Retrieved from *For Profit Higher Education: The Failure to Safeguard the Federal Investment and Ensure Student Success*, 61.

"Tell me more about that . . . ? Can you be more specific? How long has this been a problem? How do you feel about that? Have you given up trying to deal with the problem?"[30]

This process is administered for the sole purpose of atomizing the targeted lead and intended to crush an already-broken spirit. Preying upon some of the most desperate households in the country, recruiters, after having found them, berate their targets with a merciless barrage of questions, which the recruiter already knows the answers to. This conversation is by no means conducted to simply gather information or better understand the situation of the target. Based on evidence that has surfaced in recent investigations of the industry, this tactic is clearly intended to draw out the lead's vulnerability with the end purpose of beating that person into total emotional submission.

In the aftermath of being forced to recall the difficult circumstances of his or her life, a lead is then presented with a dotted line to sign. If there is resistance on behalf of the lead to sign, then the recruiter has special instructions to create a false sense of urgency to gain an immediate commitment. An example of this might be to tell the lead that there is a limited number of seats for a particular program or that they might miss the deadline to sign up if they wait. Although this is what is told to leads, this is untrue in most cases.

For instance, Apollo Group, Inc.,[31] instructs recruiters to "not tell the student we have classes running every week unless you can agree on a start date."[32] Further directions lead recruiters to say, "It looks like I might be able to squeeze you into the next start date."[33] Similarly, Career Education Corporation's,[34] "Telephone Techniques" manual directs recruiters to "limit the time-frames that you offer to a student and always express to them how busy your schedule is."[35] Bridgeport also implements this policy with their "Creating Urgency" job aid, which applies "pressure to PREVENT them from procrastinating."[36] The prevailing theme here is obvious: Recruiters are ordered to obtain an immediate commitment by any means necessary.

Given the pages from recruiters' manuals, internal memos with instructions from recruitment managers, as well as the personal testimonies of former recruiters to the HELP Committee during the two-year federal investigation of the for-profit industry, there is but one reasonable conclusion that can be drawn. Recruiters seek out and target the defenseless. Like a fox chasing a wounded bird on foot, the fate of the lead is determined far before the chase begins.

Among the most highly sought-after leads, such as unsuspecting single mothers, there are even cases of for-profit recruiters pursuing handicapped people. An uncle of a Kaplan student with cerebral palsy angrily complained to the college that his nephew, whose condition was not accommodated during his time at Kaplan, "is left with $8,400 in loans for a degree he could not possibly obtain."[37]

Already burdened by the enormous weight from the struggles of daily life, the targeted leads all but crumble under the heated pressure that is applied by an army of recruiting vultures. Although for-profit companies insist that these cases of deplorable activity are isolated to rare instances, the testimony of a former ITT recruitment manager suggests otherwise:

> In addition, at quarterly district meetings I did pain funnel training for nearly every top recruitment representative, financial aid coordinator, dean, instructor, department chairs, all functional managers, all college directors and the district manager for the entire Southern California District, the largest district in the country. The presentation material was also given out to over 100 ITT Tech employees throughout every department in the district.[38]

It seems as though the conduct in accordance to the "pain funnel," "ARTICHOKE," and others is not that of a few bad eggs at a single campus. Rather, this practice seems to have rampantly infiltrated almost every corner of every recruiting office across the country. My stepfather has eloquently expressed to me the sentiment that the greatness of a country is not found in its GDP or even in its military strength. Rather, a country's true worth can be measured by how well it cares for the weak, for the defenseless, for those who are not able to take care of themselves. The for-profits not only fail to help the disadvantaged, but they also prey upon them.

ESSENTIAL TAKEAWAYS

This chapter marks the beginning of the end for countless numbers of struggling people across the United States each year. By entering personal information into sites that promise to offer more information about college opportunities but fail to mention that their personal information is about to be sold to for-profit higher-education companies salivating at another potential client, students ultimately sign up to be berated by for-profit recruiters day in and day out.

Exposed to the most personally excruciating questions that can be crafted, a majority of leads quickly sign on to thousands of dollars of college debt under false pretenses. Although a number of vulnerable demographics, such as single mothers and people with handicaps, have been mentioned, the next chapter pays particular attention to arguably the most egregious targeting that continues to exist to this today.

3

VETERANS IN THE CROSSHAIRS

In addition to leads in general, the industry has set its sights on one group of particularly appealing targets: military servicemen and veterans. Active servicemembers, veterans, and their families have become exceedingly attractive to for-profit colleges on several financial fronts for three distinct reasons.

The first can be understood in the context that, until the latest drawback in military personnel from Iraq and Afghanistan, recent military engagements abroad have resulted in an increase of individuals entering the armed forces. Consequently, there are now more people eligible for federal military education benefits.

The second is that most of these military benefits consist of grants rather than loans. This allows students to invest in a college degree with smaller loan burdens and then pose less of a default risk to for-profit firms as a result. There is great significance to this due to the fact that notoriously high default rates on loans throughout the industry have prompted threats on behalf of the federal government to pull eligibility status for federal aid if the problem worsens. By increasing the percentage of clients who are relieved of heavier loan burdens as a result of more grant eligibility, a significant amount of the collective risk is alleviated from the industry as a whole.

Last, although military benefits still come from federal taxpayer dollars, there is a special amendment to the Higher Education Act that designates "military educational benefits" as being separate from the "Title IV education" funds that are the primary source of higher-educa-

tion funding from the federal government. This amendment was originally attached to the Higher Education Act in 1992 and provided that
Title IV funds could account for no more than 85 percent of a for-profit
institution's budget. Consequently, for-profit colleges were responsible
for covering "at least 15 percent of its revenues from sources that are
not derived from funds provided under this title, as determined in
accordance with regulations prescribed by the Secretary."[1]

However, this ratio was changed from 85/15 to 90/10 under amendments to the Higher Education Act in 1998.[2] Following a series of
readjustments to the language that regulates the calculation of these
distinct sources of revenue, the current language of the 90/10 rule
reads:

> In the case of a proprietary institution of higher education (as de-
> fined in section 1002(b) of this title), such institution will derive not
> less than ten percent of such institution's revenues from sources
> other than funds provided under this subchapter and part C of sub-
> chapter I of chapter 34 of title 42, as calculated in accordance with
> subsection (d)(1), or will be subject to the sanctions described in
> subsection (d)(2).[3]

To put it simply, a focus on people with military backgrounds helps for-
profit colleges to avoid the growing threats of regulatory restrictions
while simultaneously expanding their base of guaranteed revenue
through federal grants rather than loans.[4]

This has caused a surge in investing resources devoted to recruiting
and enrolling students eligible for military education benefits. For example, a recent Kaplan University presentation discussed plans to
"spend $29 million and hire 45 people over 3 years to enroll more
military personnel."[5] Hoping to infiltrate "key military publications and
installations," this $29 million investment would be used to establish
"broad-based outreach through phone calls, Web sites, direct-mail, and
a presence at military events."[6]

Similarly, ITT's CEO wrote in an e-mail, "We didn't even make the
top 40 providers to the military. What an opportunity that we have in
front of us," and insisted "we need to see how we can penetrate this
world."[7] However, this opportunistic attitude cannot be found in the
advertisements targeting their military audience.

A prime example of the disingenuous narrative that is typically found in such advertisements can be seen in a 2012 "ITT Tech Special Salute to Veterans" campaign. As soft piano music plays in the background and staged men and women in uniforms embrace their families after getting off the tarmac, the following narrative is read: "It took extraordinary courage, sacrifice, commitment . . . and most of all, it took hope. We want to thank all those men and women who have served our nation and helped to protect our freedom. Thank you, from all of us at ITT Technical Institute."[8]

Unbeknownst to thousands of returning veterans who watched this commercial from their living rooms, this ad was more than a simple thank-you to them. Below the shallow surface of what aired is a plan to capture a vast new market of profit. It is this potential source of revenue, and not sincere gratitude to our veterans, that has prompted new investment in the creation and airing of commercials like this one.

Among the several avenues described by Kaplan's "broad-based outreach program," websites and online lead generators stand out as one of the most effective tools to attract people with ties to the military. Among the largest companies facilitating military lead generation websites is QuinStreet, Inc., which operated such lead online sites as GI-Bill.com, Military-Net.com, and MilitaryGIBill.com. Many of these sites not only have names that make it appear as though they are facilitated by a government entity, but they also "use layouts and logos similar to official military Web sites, but do not inform users that the purpose of the site is to collect contact information on behalf of paying for-profit clients."[9] The nature of these agreements between military lead generators and for-profit colleges is validated with a "search of the VA site [which] displays a list of all 155 institutions accepting GI bill dollars for a given State. . . . Quinstreet's lead-generation site returns a list of only five schools—all for-profit colleges—representing four different companies."[10]

In the words of Kentucky Attorney General Jack Conway, "This company preyed on our veterans who received educational benefits as a result of their military service to our country," concluding that the "actions were unconscionable and purposefully drove veterans to for-profit colleges who were perhaps more interested in getting their hands on the federal benefits than in educating our soldiers and their families."[11] However, this practice was abruptly ended following a lawsuit against

QuinStreet, Inc., filed by twenty state attorneys general. In a settlement reached on June 27, 2012, QuinStreet, Inc., was forced to "turn over the Web site GIBill.com to the Department of Veterans Affairs, pay a $2.5 million fine, and fundamentally alter its disclosures on military and other Web sites."[12] Although this individual case has been settled, it highlights commonly held practices by military lead generators and the consequences that follow as a result.

Additionally, for-profit revenue is also spent on extending beyond the Internet, directly targeting Wounded Warrior centers and veterans' hospitals onsite. Bloomberg News first exposed the practice of for-profit sales pitches being directed at severely injured soldiers living in Wounded Warrior barracks. Author of the story Daniel Golden retells the account of US marine corporal James Long, a combat victim of a traumatic brain injury. Highlighting the tragedy of this story, Golden comments on the ethical problems of this case, saying that while Long "knows he's enrolled . . . he just can't remember what course he's taking."[13] This routine of seeking out wounded veterans to help boost military enrollment is, however, by no means a rare occurrence. Take Kaplan's training materials for military recruiters:

> Veterans' hospitals are another place that you can expect to find veterans. . . . many of the facilities allow schools to come on site and set up in a common area, such as a lunch room, and provide an information tables. You can expect to see not only veterans but also family members of veterans, and hospital staff that will come to your table for information.[14]

Although Kaplan denies that this document reflects the official policy on training programs approved by corporate management, it is puzzling to know that this practice has been implemented by several for-profit colleges nationwide. Grand Canyon University, for example, proves this in an exchange between a recruiter and a manager: "We were a big hit. . . . I consolidated our position with the Army National Guard at this event. . . . I also made many contacts with the wounded warrior unit. . . . I also gained 5 solid leads that will turn into applications this next week."[15]

As this series of calculated efforts are being deployed at military centers, the for-profit industry has seen a massive return on its investment. During the first two years of access to post-9/11 GI bill funds, following its passage in August 2009, eight of the top ten recipients of post-9/11 GI bill funds are for-profit education firms.[16] The Apollo Group, for example, led as the top recipient of post-9/11 GI bill benefits, with a total accumulation of $210 million over a two-year period.[17] With other major for-profit education entities, like ITT at $178 million all the way down to tenth-ranked Kaplan at $44 million, the for-profit industry has managed to capture 37 percent ($1.6 billion) of the entire military education program ($4.3 billion).[18]

While servicing only 25 percent of veterans with 37 percent of post-9/11 GI bill benefits, public schools serviced 59 percent of veterans enrolled in higher education and only received 39 percent of the benefits.[19] This means that, from a purely economic standpoint, the federal government is getting more than twice its per-dollar return on the federal subsidy of veterans enrolled in public colleges relative to veterans enrolled at for-profit colleges.

Additionally, there are two other major sources of Department of Defense (DoD) funds that flow steadily into the for-profits. The first is the Tuition Assistance (TA) program, which is available to servicemembers enrolled in postsecondary courses while still on active duty. The TA program provides a benefit of $250 per academic credit, capped at $4,500 per year, to increase servicemembers' prospects of being promoted, as well as gaining a degree which will stay with them long after their discharge from the military.[20] In the fiscal year of 2011 alone, for-profit colleges collected one of every two dollars of the Tuition Assistance Program, totaling $280 million of the $563 million allocated.[21]

A second principal fund operated by the DoD is the Military Spouse Career Advancement Accounts (MyCAA) program. The exclusive focus of this fund is to support the spouses of servicemembers in developing their career opportunities. This financial assistance is divided into increments of $2,000 per year, with an overall cap of $4,000 over the span of three years.[22] A detailed analysis of this program reveals that, during the year of 2011, for-profit colleges received $40 million of the total $65 million MyCAA program, or more than a 61 percent share of the total fund.[23] Combined, these two benefit programs represent $320 million in additional funds to for-profit institutions in a single year. Past trends indicate that these programs are continuing to climb steadily, as funds from the TA that went to for-profit colleges increased by $72 million between 2009 and 2011 (see figure 3.1).[24] As a result, it is not difficult to understand why additional military education benefit programs stand as a significant revenue source for the industry. Consequently, this fuels the sector's focus on targeting and pressuring our military servicemembers and veterans.

A sum of $1.6 billion in dependable grant money might seem like a large enough incentive on its own to devote significant resources toward securing. However, there cannot be a complete understanding of the collective motivation behind targeting servicemembers before considering the effects of the 90/10 rule. Regardless of how much federal student aid a person might qualify for, federal aid originating under Title IV of the Higher Education Act cannot exceed 90 percent of the total aid given to a student in the for-profit sector. However, educational benefits from neither the DoD nor Veterans Affairs (VA) flow from Title IV of the Higher Education Act and are completely separate.[25] Consequently, these additional military educational benefits fall on the 10 percent side of the equation, allowing many for-profit colleges to expand on their share of federal subsidies without crossing the 90/10 threshold.

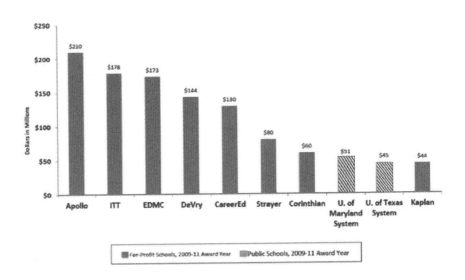

Figure 3.1.   Federal G.I. Bill Disbursements 2009–2011 *For Profit Higher Education: The Failure to Safeguard the Federal Investment and Ensure Student Success,* **Figure: Top Ten Recipients of Post-9/11 G.I. Bill Benefits, 112.**

Experts in this realm of higher education have indicated that the 90/10 rule places the interests of veterans as subordinate to the economic gains that for-profit institutions acquire as a result. In her testimony before the Subcommittee on Federal Financial Management, Government Information, Federal Services, and International Security on September 22, 2011, Ms. Hollister Petraeus, head of the Office of Servicemember Affairs at the Consumer Financial Protection Bureau, directly confronted the issue: "This loophole creates an incentive to see servicemembers as nothing more than dollar signs in uniform, and to use some very unscrupulous marketing techniques to draw them in."[26]

This focus on recruiting servicemembers and veterans as a way to fulfill a 90/10 compliance strategy can be easily seen across the industry. Bridgepoint Education, Inc.,[27] CEO Andrew Clark said in a presentation to Deutsche Bank, "We believe that when we are able to report our 90/10 for 2009, that it should decrease, and we think that decrease from 2008 will be due to our tuition assistance that our students are receiving through the military."[28] He concluded, "We've had a lot of success in that our military enrollment grew from 1% in 2007 to 17% [in] September 2009."[29]

Similarly, a July 2010 memo from a consulting company employed by at least one for-profit education company emphasized the potential revenue generation from tapping this market. Identifying military spouses as a prime source of relief to 90/10, the memo indicated that the "800,000-plus military spouses who have been authorized . . . for a one-time entitlement of up to $6,000" stand as the "most important short and long-term targets."[30] It goes on to include that "Under the most recent GI Bill, [servicemembers and veterans] can authorize up to 50 percent of his/her education benefits for the spouse to continue their education. Therefore . . . every spouse has access to two separate sources of funding."[31]

Echoing the same urgency to grow military education benefit programs, an executive from Kaplan sent out an eight-point strategies list with a heading that read, "Accelerate military billings/collections. . . . Go to D.C. and pick up the check if you have to."[32] Apparently, memos like these tend to be quite effective. From this initiative, Kaplan went on to collect $44 million in post-9/11 GI bill funds between 2009 and 2011, as well as $8.5 million in additional DoD education benefits in 2011 alone.[33]

Aside from the different marketing techniques implemented, as well as the various reasons motivating such behavior, servicemembers are often misled in regard to the comprehensiveness of military benefits. Although GI bill funds are a source of significant aid for servicememebers and veterans around the country, some institutions are not eligible for these programs. However, there is substantial evidence that recruiters for these ineligible institutions lull veterans into committing to for-profit colleges through false statements concerning eligibility.

Take the story of Army Staff Sergeant Jon Elliot, who, upon his return from Iraq, decided to invest in an education at ATI Career Center in Texas. Painfully recounting his story, Elliot explained, "I was assured over the phone that . . . they had been accepted back in April for the Post-9/11 program. I went in, did a face-to-face with a recruitment official. Once again I asked, 'Are you sure we're good for the Post-9/11?' He said, 'Yes' and we started doing some paperwork."[34]

To Sgt. Elliot's dismay, he was notified three months later by the Department of Veterans Affairs that ATI was "not an authorized institution of higher education, and no benefits would be paid."[35] Unfortunately, "Sgt. Elliot could not afford to pay the tuition without using his benefits, dropped out of school, and was subsequently pursued by ATI for the $9,600 that he had been told the GI Bill would pay for."[36]

Although ATI ultimately forgave the debt in this particular case after it gained significant media attention from testimony in a Senate HELP Committee hearing, less fortunate veterans from every corner of the country continue to face similar practices. As Ms. Hollister Petraeus recently wrote in a piece to the *New York Times*, the practice "does a disservice to veterans and taxpayers alike."[37]

ESSENTIAL TAKEAWAYS

Aside from targeting average Americans, many of whom find themselves in positions of financial and emotional vulnerability, for-profit colleges have made it a practice to prey upon the men and women who have bravely fought to defend our nation. Employing the same predatory recruiting techniques as they do to average citizens, for-profit colleges promote phony lead generator websites and administer high-pressure sales tactics at military hospitals.

Practices such as these have been employed not only to gain more than $1.6 billion in additional federal grants but also in an effort to offset a strict 90/10 rule on the ratio of money that can be accepted through Title IV of the Higher Education Act. The for-profit higher-education sector is no stranger to committing offenses against its students and taxpayers. However, I consider their treatment of the men and women who have sacrificed to preserve our way of life to be the worst offense of them all.

4

FILLING THE GAP OR FILLING SEATS?

"There's a gap in America between the skills we have and the skills employers need. Solving that is our highest priority."[1] In this September 2012 advertisement, the University of Phoenix encapsulates what they *claim* to be not only their mission but that of the entire industry as well. In their mission statement, "University of Phoenix provides access to higher education opportunities that enable students to develop knowledge and skills necessary to achieve their professional goals" in addition to "facilitating cognitive and affective student learning—knowledge, skills, and values—and to promote use of that knowledge in the student's work place."[2] Ashford University echoes this language with their own mission in "providing accessible, affordable, innovative, high-quality learning opportunities and degree programs . . . in which students gain knowledge and build skills and values useful in their personal and career development."[3]

For decades, for-profits have emphasized their unique position in the college market. Separate from traditional four-year and even two-year programs in the nonprofit higher-education sector, for-profit colleges have claimed to offer programs with a strong focus on the transition from the classroom to the workforce. DeVry, for example, recently ran a bus shelter advertisement campaign with the following emphasis: "John doesn't need to take the bus anymore because he was given the company car after he got a job with a big-time contractor because he studied game and simulation programming at DeVry University."[4] From these types of advertisements, for-profit colleges insist that there is a particular focus on relevant job market skills, as well as sufficient student and career services staff who are ready to support such a transition.

Although these mission statements promise adequate student support that will translate quickly into employment, their practices fail to fulfill these stated commitments. From data collected in 2010 on the for-profit colleges that were under investigation by the Senate HELP Committee and GAO, the relevant firms employed 35,202 recruiters, compared to 12,452 student support staff and only 3,512 career services staff.[5] To put this into more understandable terms, there were an average of 44 students per recruiter, compared to 125 students per student support staff member and 455 students per career services employee.

There is another factor that makes these figures even more troubling. As enrollment soared by more than 700,000 students between 2007 and 2010, the number of recruiters increased by roughly 14,000, or 67 percent from 2007.[6] Compared to this significant increase, student services only grew by approximately 3,000 employees, or 25 percent, and career services did not see any measurable increase at all.[7] These figures demonstrate the association in the upward trend of both recruiters and enrollment.[8]

A comparison of the mission statement at the University of Phoenix with the type of personnel it has invested in certainly illustrates an inconsistency between what is promised to students and what is actually available. The employment records of its holding company, Apollo Group, Inc., show that in 2010 Apollo employed 3,737 student services staff, compared to 8,137 recruiters, while also employing 1,140 full-time faculty, compared to 31,671 part-time faculty.[9] Yet, a portion of the University of Phoenix's mission includes evaluating "student learning and using assessment data to improve the teaching/learning system, curriculum, instruction, learning resources, counseling and student services."[10] How can the University of Phoenix possibly claim that part of their mission is to "improve the teaching/learning system, curriculum, instruction, learning resources, counseling and student services," while Apollo employed more than twice the number of recruiters than student services personnel and nearly twenty-eight times the number of part-time faculty relative to full-time faculty? As we have seen, it appears as though the "number one priority" of for-profit colleges is to maximize enrollment, not to equip students with the tools and support necessary to obtain a job.

In addition to the data, numerous documented complaints filed with every major for-profit college under investigation also help to support this conclusion. In a formal complaint filed by an Ashford University student to its holding company of Bridgepoint Education, Inc., the student explained how the shortages in student services staff affect students once they are enrolled: "When I was enrolling in classes, I had no problems with someone from the school returning my phone call. . . . Now that I am an existing student, I cannot get anyone to return my phone calls."[11]

It is a classic bait and switch. Luring students to commit with an onslaught of peppy slogans and high-pressure sales tactics, for-profit colleges continue to stun hundreds of thousands of students each year by delivering virtually nothing of substance in the long term. In the words of a former ITT student, "In so many ways, I feel like my life's dream has been ripped right out of my hands."[12] The inherent flaws of the for-profit system adequately account for why these problems emerge. For-profit colleges simply use the idea of education as a means to generate profit.

Under this established framework, for-profit colleges focus a high amount of revenue and resources into their recruitment offices to reach maximum levels of enrollment. Simultaneously, the students who are now committed to the programs attempt to learn in a world with little to no investment in student or career services. Why? Because for-profits simply view students not as investments but as cash cows. Therefore, once the herd has been guided into its pen, there is no incentive on behalf of the college to offer the programs and services that were promised.

This low investment in student and career services staff has consequently led to prevailingly poor academic quality of its programs. This is particularly the case for online programs, which many for-profit colleges invest heavily in because they offer broad access and can be operated cheaply.

Take one of the industry's largest firms, Bridgepoint Education, Inc., which is the parent company of Ashford University and the University of the Rockies. From their two "campuses," which are little more than headquarter offices, 99 percent of the students are exclusively enrolled in online programs.[13] Interestingly, Bridgepoint also leads the industry in associate degree withdrawal rates at 84 percent.[14]

The correlating rates of high online enrollment and high withdrawal rates are by no means coincidental. As the industry pushes toward a higher concentration of online programs, cheaper for the college to operate and more appealing to a wider customer base of students, industry-wide withdrawal rates are progressively trending upward as a result.

So why exactly are for-profit colleges, particularly the online programs they administer, lacking in academic rigor? To find out, undercover employees from the GAO enrolled in twelve different online colleges with fake identities and academic transcripts.[15] Associated with the astronomical withdrawal rates, the likely causes for deficient academic rigor were revealed from these random accounts in 2011.

From their findings, the GAO concluded, "the course structure across the schools consists of self-directed reading from books and Web sites, online discussion-threads, online tests, individual written assignments or power-points, and a few courses that included group assignments."[16] The GAO goes on to further add, "the discussions look like what one might expect from an online blog or social networking site."[17]

Even more troubling than the lack of substance of these discussions is the typical weight they held in the course grade. On average, these online chat exchanges were worth between 10 percent and 40 percent of the cumulative class grade.[18] Furthermore, additional questions have been raised about the legitimacy of the online curriculum at these colleges, following a closer examination of the range of required intro-level courses, as well as their substance.

During their undercover enrollment, GAO employees were required to enroll in a mishmash of basic courses ranging from three to six weeks and costing thousands of dollars for no apparent purpose or academic gain.[19] A selection of these mandatory courses includes "Introduction to the Criminal Justice Program," "Introductory Computing," "Introduction to Paralegal Studies," "Introductory Math," "Critical Thinking," "Introduction to Medical Billing," "Keyboarding," and "Learning Strategies and Techniques."[20] Although basic-level courses, which are intended to introduce students to a variety of topics, are mandatory at many traditional colleges across the country, this list takes that concept to an absurd level.

Conventionally, an introductory-level course requirement is intended to equip students with a variety of tools necessary to excel in other courses later on in college. Indeed, Ashford University claims that their online programs are consistent with this mission in providing "foundational perspective, breadth, and professional relevance for undergraduate and graduate students." It would be difficult to assert, however, that this is the purpose behind requiring "Introduction to Medical Billing," just to list one example.

With the traditional justification for such basic courses ruled out, there is but one reasonable explanation for such requirements. By forcing students to enroll in several introductory-level classes at several thousand dollars apiece, this stands as a highly effective way of generating additional revenue quickly and easily.

In response to this accusation, a for-profit college might claim that, although their model may have more variety in what they require compared to other colleges, there is still academic merit and practical purpose behind such a curriculum. Two fundamental facts repudiate this response. The first of these, coming from the GAO investigation, emphasizes the deficiency of both the material being taught as well as the incompetence of the instructors teaching it. It reveals that many of these introductory classes tested students on material that was much too basic for a college course.

For example, one "Introductory Computing" quiz question to a GAO agent was "When entering text within a document, you normally press Enter at the end of every _____," with possible answers including: "page, sentence, line, and paragraph."[21] Surely, questions of this nature are so rudimentary that they promote neither well-roundness nor substantive thought, and yet this is the level of assessment being proctored for sums in the thousands of dollars. As one ITT student put it, "I was rather frustrated with the class I took, and felt that I learned nothing and do not feel a bill for $2,500 is a fair amount to be paying for a rather inadequate education."[22]

Besides the material itself being classified by many students as "inadequate," there were also complaints of the faculty being equally disappointing. "The complete and total lack of preparation, effort, and desire to perform on the part of the instructor has made this course, without any doubt in my mind, the largest waste of time, money, effort, and resources since I have begun attending this school."[23] Sharing the sentiments of this ITT student is another from Herzing,[24] who wrote, "we are currently in our fourth week of class and . . . I can honestly say that I have not learned anything in this class," further commenting that the instructor was unable to answer questions on a consistent basis.[25] Students from UTI[26] recount similar stories in being self-taught without any direction from the instructor whatsoever:

> What I've gathered in my first course is that it appears I've indebted myself $15k dollars to show up in uniform and decipher procedures from a service manual, basically teaching myself instead of receiving accurate and consistent direction from an instructor regarding practical, procedural instruction. . . . the fact that he was left to instruct us without having a demonstrable mastery of all the concepts and procedures covered is something I can't comprehend or ignore without critique.[27]

A Kaplan student best captures what seems to be the general consensus from former students in the for-profit industry: "This is a corporate run school and as such . . . Money is the main object, not the quality of the education provided."[28] Echoing my earlier assertions that for-profit colleges are inherently flawed, the internal complaints and personal testimonies of countless former students illustrate the shortcomings of both the curriculum and instruction at many of these for-profit colleges.

Additionally, even with such incredibly low standards, students who failed to meet the bar were often offered several chances to "retake the same test" and earn credit.[29] For example, one GAO employee who enrolled at Career Point received an e-mail from his teacher that read, "Those assignments you did not pass, I've opened them up so you can retake them. They are open book so there should not be any failure. All answers are right in the book and there is no time limit."[30] Not only are students oftentimes allowed to retake exams with an open-book option, but also there is little investment in tutoring services that would most likely help these students in their performance.

For example, one Kaplan student filed a complaint concerning the "academic success center," which advertises that it "offers assistance with writing, math, and science."[31] While this is what was marketed, the center did not employ a single tutor in any of the advertised areas of study.[32] Similarly, a former Herzing student submitted a virtually identical complaint, explaining that he was "absolutely astonished by the lack of communication, lack of effort, and lack of support" that he had received during his enrollment as a student.[33]

Instead of channeling resources into student services programs intended to tutor and assist students in actual academic growth, for-profits notoriously take the cheaper and less-demanding route of offering students multiple open-book exam retakes and a low-rigor curriculum. From this, student growth is minimal, while the cost of attendance is high. The only party that benefits under this model is the for-profit institution, which increases their bottom line by saving money with reduced operating costs.

To summarize, enrolled students are forced to take a variety of random, low-rigor courses from ineffective instructors. As a result, some students fail to meet the fairly lowly set bar due to the circumstances surrounding the learning environment. For these students, several test retakes are offered with an open-book rule. Considering these circumstances, how can students possibly, in the words of University of Phoenix's mission statement, "develop knowledge and skills necessary to achieve their professional goals, improve the productivity of their organizations and provide leadership and service to their communities?"[34] How can we possibly expect the student products of these programs to be capable of "leading" once these pathetic standards are removed upon entering the real world?

Astoundingly, testimony from former faculty members at for-profit colleges reveal that this problem is even worse than it appears. Not only do many professors across the industry allow students to operate under such free and minimal conditions, but administrators also often instruct teachers to not fail students who should have and otherwise would. In the words of an instructor at the UTI-owned campus NTI:

> We at NTI are being told to pass students who should fail because we are "training entry level technicians who paid for the certificates like everybody else." I am sorry if this offends you, but I was under the impression that our students paid for an education, not just a piece of paper!! I have been told to give students points to pass my courses when they should fail.[35]

As the professor goes on to conclude, graduates from institutions that notoriously condone these practices are not taken seriously when applying for a job. "Every day that I come to work, I hear students tell me that they have encountered employers that point blank tell them that they do not hire NTI students because of consistent poor performance." It is not difficult to understand, bearing in mind the laundry list of flaws just outlined, why employers would avoid graduates of for-profit colleges.

Considering this report from the GAO, it is difficult to take institutions like Kaplan seriously when their mission statements promise such outcomes as "applied scholarship in a practical environment."[36] How exactly do the findings from the GAO report reflect either scholarship or a practical environment? This cannot possibly be considered an adequate return for such a serious investment, particularly when 86 percent of it is paid for with taxpayer dollars.

The second reason for-profit colleges are not legitimately invested in offering a quality education comes from the report findings that prove several cases of blatantly accepted plagiarized work. During their investigation, GAO employees enrolled in five different classes at Rasmussen University and Corinthian-owned Everest University.[37] Throughout the courses, GAO employees purposefully submitted work that was recognizably plagiarized on multiple occasions, either by copying and pasting from common Internet sources or submitting identical work.[38]

Four of the five cases granted full or partial credit for the assignments, two of the instructors never acknowledged the offense in any way, and neither of the colleges enforced its own academic honesty policy in response to the violation.[39] Hence, the apathetic nature of for-profit colleges toward its students in the plagiarism cases remains consistent with the substandard trend of the industry as a whole.

Aside from the questionable rigor at many of these institutions, which arguably plays a part in deterring employers from hiring for-profit graduates at significant rates, there is another factor that continues to promote poor student outcomes. Despite an inadequate investment in career services throughout the industry, prospective students at for-profit colleges are led to believe that there is a high focus on the transition between a degree and job placement.

Advertisements like the DeVry bus campaign or the September 2012 University of Phoenix "Let's Get to Work, America" television commercial are among the best examples of this. However, relevant statistics and testimony surrounding this investment solidifies that such sales pitches are neither factual nor genuine. Supporting this assertion is the average ratio of students to career services staff, which reached up to 1,545 students per career services employee.[40]

One of the worst offenders in this regard is Bridgepoint-owned Ashford University, which serviced their 77,179 students in the fall of 2010 with only a single career placement advisor.[41] Even more extreme is the Apollo-owned University of Phoenix, which had a fall 2010 ratio of 470,800 students to 0 career services staff.[42] So how exactly does the University of Phoenix expect to "get America back to work" without the presence of a career services office for student job placement?

Kathleen Bittel, a career services employee at the EDMC-owned Art Institute online division, confirms these statistics with her own experience at EDMC: "I see a systematic problem when there are only nine employees servicing students that are being recruited by an admissions workforce of almost 1,600."[43] She further adds, "Career Services employees are being paid nearly a third of what the top performers in the admission department receive. I believe that these facts speak volumes as to where the real priorities lie within these companies."[44]

Operating under Bittel's supposition surrounding different financial investments in the various servicing offices, the poor quality of the few student and career resources that do exist quickly come into focus. As a Concorde student explained in a formal complaint, "it was made to sound like they had connections for a graduate at any point in their career as long as they asked for help." However, most of the "job placement" networking the school does is through websites like Craig's List and Monster, sites that anyone with a computer has access to.[45]

To no surprise, the criminal justice department chair at the California-based UEI College explains the difficulty that virtually all of his students face in the job market: "So far, I believe none of my former CJ [criminal justice] students have been able to obtain a job in the field."[46] Sadly, I remain unsurprised by this testimony. When a career services staff member who is overwhelmed by hundreds or even thousands of students is limited to Craig's List for networking resources, it becomes clear why so many for-profit graduates struggle to find employment.

ESSENTIAL TAKEAWAYS

Lured into applying through deceptive advertisements, for-profit colleges engage in a blatant bait-and-switch tactic of promising strong student and career services that will equip students with the skills necessary to be successful in the job market. Instead, for-profit colleges invest a disproportionately high amount of its resources into recruiting as a way to sustain and grow enrollment while seriously neglecting the services that were promised. Consequently, many students perform poorly as a direct result of insufficient academic programs. In an attempt to raise student performance, for-profit colleges often lower the level of rigor, which then deters employers from hiring graduates from these programs, crippling students as a result.

5

COOKING THE BOOKS

It has been established that, from the combination of minimal career services staff and the limited resources available to students, job placement is among the lowest of priorities in the for-profit sector. If for-profit colleges value student post-graduation performance so little, then why are *any* resources given to student and career services at all?

The answer lies in an incentive to capture a baseline quota percentage. If job placement figures drop below a certain level, colleges face the risk of losing their federal aid eligibility status. As a result, executives reward placement counselors who reach their quotas with massive bonuses, as was the case with Kathleen Bittel earning a potential 33 percent bonus upon meeting an 85.9 percent job placement percentage rate.[1] If employers are not hiring for-profit graduates, then how exactly do career advisors meet job placement targets? The answer is simple; for-profit colleges simply distort reality in order to inflate the actual employment rates.

Generally, the first step is to eliminate certain graduates from the "not employed" calculation altogether. For example, military spouses and stay-at-home parents are eligible for exemption under the technical definitions of *employment*. As a result, it is easier to just remove these graduates immediately instead of investigating whether they hold jobs.[2] Moreover, "established professionals" employed in unrelated fields are also eligible for exclusion from official calculations.

Another key exemption embraced by many for-profits is the placement exception for graduates "pursuing further education."[3] As a result, for-profit colleges are infamously known to promote additional programs to graduates with the intent of significantly growing this portion of students. In an exchange between campus directors at Kaplan University, one director asked, "John, I was wondering if you could send a list of your MA and MOS graduates from the last 2 years, so we can reach out to them to offer the MPM Associate Degree Program. . . . this will help you with your placement numbers since they will be continuing school."[4]

If a student does not qualify for exemption under the quota, placement counselors are then charged with the task of finding a way to count their graduates as being employed in their fields of study. According to Kathleen Bittel's testimony to the Senate HELP Committee, EDMC employees "were expected to convince graduates that skills they used in jobs such as working as waiters, payroll clerks, retail sales, and gas station attendants were actually related to their course of study in areas like graphic design and residential planning."[5]

Upon being swayed, graduates would then consent to sign documents that claimed them to be employed in their fields. Internal ITT documents reveal how incredibly flexible the criteria are for defining employment in a related field. The manual definition requires only 20 percent to 49 percent of time spent on the job using the skills taught by core classes as being necessary to qualify as employed in a "related field."[6]

A Senate HELP Committee investigation suggests that, before Blockbuster closed its remaining stores in January 2014, "under this criteria an employee at Blockbuster, for example, could qualify as being employed in the field of digital entertainment and game design programming."[7] From these loose definitions, for-profit colleges are able to drastically inflate their job placement rates. This not only solidifies federal education aid eligibility status, but it also allows colleges to mislead prospective students across the country with the thought that, by attending a for-profit college, you are virtually guaranteed a secure path to a career.

Similar to the ITT documents are circumstances surrounding one of the industry's other largest firms, Education Management Corp. (EDMC), which owns and operates the College of Art Institutes, Brown Mackie College, Argosy University, and South University Online. In a November 2012 story that aired on ABC News, former

EDMC employee-turned-whistleblower Jason Sobek provides firsthand insight into exactly how for-profits cook the books on job placement.[8] Backed by internal documents containing figures on each student, including their employment status, the income from that employment, and so on, Sobek concludes that EDMC "manipulated the job placement rates by counting students working in a job that they did not need the degree for. In my opinion, it's a wretched fraud."[9]

One victim of this misleading system is single mother Sarah Fisher, a graduate of EDMC's business management program at Brown Mackie College in South Bend, Indiana.[10] During an interview, she told ABC News that "they [Brown Mackie College] told me I'd be making $35,000 to $40,000 a year."[11] During her schooling, Fisher took a job at Walmart in order to help support her children, making $16,000 a year.[12] Although she took the job long before she graduated, Brown Mackie College still counts her customer service job as "related" to her business management degree.[13]

This case alone presents two very large problems, the first being harm to the individual. For Fisher and her family, the business management degree from Brown Mackie has been outcompeted in the job market by other applicants with degrees from schools that are far more reputable. As a result, Fisher is "about $24,000 in the hole for a degree [she] can't use."[14] This leaves a single mother struggling to support her family in a precarious situation because her degree not only fails to make her more competitive in the job market, but she is also now struggling to pay off a $24,000 student debt with interest compounding every day.

The second problem considers the more collective component of its impact on society in terms of its effect on prospective students. Fisher's story is technically considered in EDMC's job placement data as being a success. From Sobek's leaked documents concerning EDMC job placement reports, Sarah Fisher's customer service job at Walmart is "related" to her degree.[15] Despite the significantly lower pay scale than originally promised and the fact that she attained the job well before her graduation from Brown Mackie, EDMC can still advertise Sarah Fisher as a statistic that has been helped rather than harmed by her education at Brown Mackie College. Consequently, Fisher has become one of countless statistics that has been manipulated to mislead prospective students with misrepresented data. Sobek explains that this is a

common practice, conducted with the "purpose of marketing job placement success rates to potential students."[16]

In addition to EDMC job placement data, deceptive employment
rate inflation techniques can be found throughout the industry. Considered to be "employed in a related field" by for-profit firms, additional
cases of graduates deemed to be a success span from a graduate with a
fashion design degree who now sells shoes to an accounting graduate
who works as a McDonald's cashier.[17] This has inevitably created a false
sense of job security for prospective students, thus sustaining the high
volume of student input into the industry as a result. Validating this
assertion, Sobek explains that such tactics are deployed in an "intention-
al business model" as a way to attract applicants.[18]

Trends further demonstrate that this technique stands as a highly
effective tool to recruit students and generate profit, given that more
than 1.6 million students were likely to have been influenced by such
tactics in the fiscal year of 2010 alone. EDMC offered a response to
Sobek's allegations, saying, "We believe that the claims raised [by Jason
Sobek] are wholly without merit."[19] This, however, is confusing. If his
claims, based on the data accessed from internal EDMC databases, are
"wholly without merit," what exactly fails to hold merit? Are the numbers wrong? Has Sarah Fisher gained employment in a field other than
her $16,000-a-year customer-service job at Walmart? Has she been
hired as a professional in business management with the $35,000-to-
$40,000 salary that she was promised by Brown Mackie recruiters? If
not, was she accidentally listed as having been hired in a "related" field,
or does EDMC honestly consider her current condition a success story?
As Senator Dick Durbin comments to ABC News, "It's just plain
fraud."[20]

Thus far, a compelling case has been built against the genuine motive of for-profit firms and their mission of serving as a pathway to
employment. However, there is an additional problem that has become
increasingly prevalent, in that many for-profit programs across the
country are not accredited by state licensing organizations.

The relevance of this problem begins with the framework of individual states establishing a series of occupational licensing boards. These
committees oversee occupations requiring licenses, ranging from the
American Bar Association for attorneys to the Commission on Accreditation of Allied Health Education Programs for diagnostic sonogra-

phers.[21] Combined, experts suggest that "at least a fifth, and perhaps as much as a third, of the work force is directly affected by licensing laws."[22]

While traditional colleges virtually never face problems meeting these standards, many for-profit colleges function under a vastly different set of circumstances. This model consists of programmatic accreditation and licensure, in the sense that, while some programs are recognized as being accredited, other programs, as well as the college as a whole, are not.[23] Under this system, two major hazards stand in the way of students enrolled in the nonaccredited programs. Either "students often cannot find work because employers only hire graduates from accredited programs, or, because State laws prohibit graduates from non-accredited programs from practicing their specialty."[24] Thus, unbeknownst to students enrolled in these programs, any time and money spent earning these degrees is essentially all but wasted.

Testimony from Yasmine Issa, a former student of Sanford-Brown College, which is owned and operated by Career Education Corporation (CEC), provides insight into one of the nation's leading offenders in regard to administering degree programs that have little to no possibility of being recognized by the law or employers. At the expense of $32,000, Issa completed an eighteen-month sonography program with the intention of working in an obstetrical office and performing ultrasounds upon her graduation in 2008.[25]

Following graduation, Issa was informed by prospective employers that, before her application could be considered, she needed to complete a licensing examination in order to be certified by the American Registry for Diagnostic Medical Sonographers (ARDMS).[26] To Issa's astonishment, the Sanford-Brown sonography program was not programmatically accredited, barring Issa from sitting for the exam.[27] Reflecting on the difficult situation she faced after learning about the accrediting problems, Issa explains, "I thought that going to school to learn a marketable skill would allow me to provide for my family. Instead, it has left me more than $20,000 in debt and unable to be hired in the field I trained for."[28]

Echoing the experience of Ms. Issa is the case of Eric Schmitt, a graduate of Kaplan University's nonaccredited paralegal studies program. While earning an associate's degree in paralegal studies, Schmitt was assured that, upon his graduation from the program, he would have the opportunity to go on to earn a law degree by enrolling in Concord Law School, also owned by Kaplan Higher Education.[29] Cases of such encouragement have become progressively common by for-profit firms, largely in an industry-wide attempt to keep unemployment figures of graduates low through the technique of factoring students into the "pursuing further education" category.[30]

While Schmitt testified that it appeared as though "Kaplan could provide everything [he] needed to fulfill [his] dream of practicing law,"[31] Kaplan arguably had little capacity to help Schmitt reach this goal in reality. What Kaplan did have to offer Schmitt was a nonaccredited paralegal studies program and a relatively low first-time California bar–passing rate of 37.1 percent at Concord Law School, compared to the average first-time California bar–passing rate of approximately 55 percent.[32] Additionally, Kaplan also holds the third-highest associate's-degree-withdrawal rate of major for-profit companies at a staggering 69 percent.[33] Considering each of these factors, Mr. Schmitt and countless others at Kaplan are set up for failure right from the very beginning.

Unfortunately, these accounts from Sanford-Brown and Kalpan are by no means isolated. In her testimony to the Senate HELP Committee, retired Iowa Department of Education administrator Arlie Thoreson Willems recounted a substantial number of cases from students across the country.[34] With a majority of complaints traced back to former students of Ashford University, Willems describes that countless students told of being misled by Ashford's recruiters on matters regarding accreditation eligibility.[35] Thousands of calls from students around the country were ultimately directed to Willems in the Iowa Department of Education because Ashford operates a single, small physical campus located in Iowa, while 99 percent of their students are exclusively enrolled in online programs that service students in every corner of the country.[36] After collecting information from thousands of complaint cases, Willems found that, under occupational licensing codes, many degrees from Ashford were not accepted by state licensing boards throughout the country. "In order to work as elementary school teachers," for example, "students attending Ashford had to participate in an approved clinical program from another college."[37] In essence, elementary teaching certification from an online program at Ashford University is practically worthless because that certification is invalid without an additional clinical program that can only be obtained at another college.

One dismayed Ashford student from Kansas expressed, "I was really blown away to find out that I had spent so much time and money at a college that I was not going to be able to obtain my Teacher's license from. The only reason I left my other college was because I was told that I would be able to receive my Teacher's license from Ashford."[38] A similar complaint, this time from a former Kaplan student, reveals similar levels of deception regarding programmatic accreditation:

> I started attending Kaplan Career Institute in February of 2007. I noted the overly eager sales representative who reeled me in. . . . I was told by the instructors that the classes we were taking were going to count towards our licensing as electricians, but later down the road I began to hear differently. The School is accredited by the state, but the Electrician program was not recognized by the Electrical board.[39]

From a large collection of nondisclosed programmatic accreditation information, internal complaints, and several testimonies from former dissatisfied students and Department of Education officials, only one conclusion can be drawn. This deceptive practice is rampant throughout the country, misleading thousands of students to waste their time and money each year. Under programmatic accreditation standards, many students are neither accepted by employers as credible applicants nor permitted by state licensing boards to practice in the intended fields of employment. In other words, it is a lose-lose situation for countless students enrolled in the for-profit higher-education sector.

ESSENTIAL TAKEAWAYS

Each year, tens of billions of taxpayer dollars are ultimately funneled to advertising and profit rather than instruction. The subsequent lack of student support and career services staff that is vital to a complete transition into the workforce has resulted in high withdrawal rates, low graduation levels, and abysmal employment figures in recent years.

To compensate, many placement counselors, acting under the pressures of quota systems passed down by executives, inflate job placement rates using a series of methods. This not only gives students a false sense of eventual job security, but it also enables colleges to remain eligible for federal grants and loans that would otherwise be withheld if job data did not include underemployment that has been manipulated to appear as "employed in a related field." Additionally, many students never even have the chance to reach the interview process, given the fact that a large number of students are enrolled in nonaccredited programs that do not grant them eligibility to sit for licensing exams.

This ultimately creates an entire class of people who are collectively no better off than they were before their time at the for-profit college, leaving with large sums of debt and no useful degree to show for it. Consequently, there is more of a burden than a benefit to students and taxpayers who see little to no return on their investment in the for-profit sector.

6

LENDING LIES

Up to this point, the claimed motives, ethical standards, and tangible benefits within for-profit colleges have been discredited. The preceding chapters have explained what is available and how it is offered at for-profit colleges. Moving on from the previous chapters, which cover what students are *receiving* at for-profit institutions, this chapter examines what students are *paying* for these services. This is particularly important because, as an industry that receives 86 percent of its funds from federal taxpayer money, or approximately $32 billion in 2010 alone, the for-profit industry is hardly privately financed (see figure 6.1).[1] As a result, a careful cost-benefit analysis must be applied when evaluating the for-profit market.

So far, we have analyzed and come to the conclusion that the benefit side of this equation is significantly low in terms of what students gain. As the evidence suggests, an investment in a for-profit higher education not only fails to deliver tangible returns to students and taxpayers alike, but it also has proven to be a very expensive investment relevant to its nonproprietary counterparts.

In regard to certificate programs, associate degrees, and bachelor degrees, for-profit colleges have proven to be consistently more expensive than nonprofit public colleges. While a certificate program at a public college costs an average of $4,249, for-profit colleges charge more than four times that, with an average cost of $19,806.[2] As for four-year bachelor degree programs, while the average cost at a public school amounts to $52,522, the average cost to students for the same

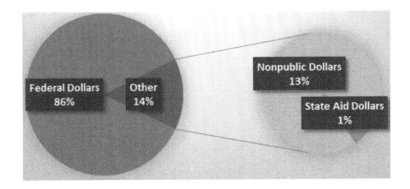

Figure 6.1. Breakdown of Revenue to For-Profit Higher Education. *For Profit Higher Education: The Failure to Safeguard the Federal Investment and Ensure Student Success,* **Figure: Revenue Collected by 15 Publicly Traded For-Profit Education Companies, 25.**

degree at a for-profit college costs an average of $62,702.[3] However, the most staggering price differential between public colleges and for-profit colleges can be found among associate degree programs. While the cost of an associate degree at a public college totals an average of $8,313, an associate degree at a for-profit college costs $34,988, or almost $27,000 more than its public counterpart.[4] For example, Strayer University, based out of Arlington, VA, charges approximately $36,500 to students enrolled in associate degree programs.[5] Relative to Strayer, Northern Virginia Community College, its public alternative located in the same area, charges $9,587 for its associate degree programs.[6] Ultimately, these figures represent a price gap of 281 percent.

While these statistics are reflective of the average price difference, other smaller variances exist as well. Such examples include the comparison between American Public University (for-profit) and Blue Ridge Community College (nonprofit), both based out of the same region in West Virginia. While an associate degree program at American Public University costs $15,250, Blue Ridge Community College charges $8,900 for its associate degree programs.[7] This difference accounts for a price gap of only 71 percent.

However, there are also cases of substantially higher price differences between sectors as well. In Colorado, for example, Westwood College charges $48,194 for associate degrees, while the same program at the Community College of Denver only costs $8,823.[8] This represents a 446 percent price discrepancy. Although there are variances in the degree of difference between for-profit programs and comparable degrees at public colleges, one thing is absolutely certain: For-profit colleges are regularly and unequivocally more expensive than their public counterparts (see figure 6.2).

There is a particularly important reason I compare for-profit colleges with public institutions and not private nonprofit universities. This is because the proposals that I lay out in chapter 10 are directly tied to public schools, particularly community colleges while having virtually nothing to do with nonprofit private universities. By contrasting the two in the way that I have, the beginning stages of offering a cheaper and more efficient alternative are established.

With that said, for-profit institutions are funded in drastically different ways. While public colleges are directly subsidized by the government, private institutions, both for-profit and nonprofit, are not. However, framing the funding distinctions between these institutional categories in this way is not entirely accurate. While 86 percent of the private for-profit sector is funded through grants and loans provided by the federal government, private nonprofits receive only a fraction of these funds. This places for-profit universities in closer financial proximity to public institutions than private nonprofit colleges. Ultimately, these two factors make a public-to-for-profit comparison more relevant than a nonprofit-to-for-profit comparison.

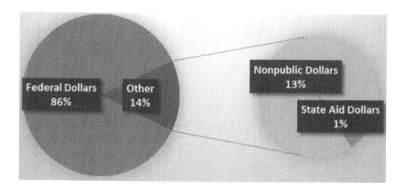

Figure 6.2.   Average Tuition Rate Comparison. *For Profit Higher Education: The Failure to Safeguard the Federal Investment and Ensure Student Success,* **Figure: Average Tuition and Fees at For-Profit and Public Colleges, 36. See Appendix 14 for a complete list of programs and tuition.**

Having already examined the way revenue is divided by expenditure at for-profit colleges, with an average of only 17 percent being allocated to instruction, it is reasonable to suspect that these significantly higher tuition rates are not being generated for any sort of student benefit. With this being the case, why are for-profit institutions consistently more expensive than public colleges? Internal memos from executives at several major for-profit colleges reveal that pricing decisions are made to maximize revenue under obligations to company shareholders and are based on the internal financial projections of the company rather than on the cost of educating students.[9]

As a report filed with the Senate HELP Committee suggests, although recent price hikes at public colleges have largely been based on state budget cuts, "tuition increases at for-profit colleges are not driven solely by external economic pressures, nor are they tempered by internal cost-saving measures, but rather, are often the result of strategies designed to maximize revenue."[10] With a motive established, what exactly is the process by which for-profit colleges attempt to maximize revenue?

From data trends, for-profit institutions appear to measure available federal aid as a generic benchmark for tuition levels. First-year students who apply for federal aid as independents, meaning financially self-dependent, are eligible for up to $9,500 in federal Stafford loans, while Pell grant recipients can gain up to an additional $3,705.[11] As a result, many of the prospective students who are recruited by for-profit colleges hold a value of $13,205 in guaranteed revenue generation from federal aid. In addition to major for-profit colleges charging a bare minimum tuition that matches this federal aid value, a 2012 National Bureau of Economic Research study found that "for profit colleges receiving Federal student aid funds charged far more tuition than those that were not eligible to receive federal aid."[12]

Interestingly enough, following congressional measures taken in 2008 to raise the Stafford loan limit to $9,500, Bridgepoint-owned Ashford University raised its tuition and technology fee to a joint total of $9,486.[13] It just so happens that this new Ashford University rate was only $14 under the cap of $9,500 in newly available student loans. Like Bridgepoint, internal documents from Atla, Inc., indicate that executives considered ways to restructure its programs so that the company was able to collect as much revenue from federal aid as possible. A 2009 pricing strategy document illustrates this phenomenon in action, as it recommends the company to "restructure terms to 3 trimesters/year or quarter time so that we can grab more of the students' Stafford."[14] Additionally, the study also found that tuition premiums, charged by for-profit colleges that are eligible for Title IV program funds, were almost identical to the average amount of revenue spent to recruit each student at for-profit colleges.[15]

Additionally, internal Bridgepoint documents also reveal the technique of matching tuition with Title IV student aid. Soon after the 2008 congressional changes were put into effect, Bridegepoint created a new fee for a majority of its courses called the "Course Digital Materials" fee, which shifted the total cost of attendance to roughly $400 above the $9,500 Stafford loan limit.[16] Alarmed after being notified of this $400 gap, Bridegepoint's CEO Andrew Clark e-mailed his CFO, "The tuition increase for bachelor degree students is going to cause a $400 short fall!!! People are talking about crazy stuff like alternative financing. You told me there would be no short fall!"[17] In his response, the CFO reassured Clark that the shortfall was a result of the fees: "With this increase and one additional increase, we can still say that our 'tuition' is below title 4 limits at every grade level."[18] This internal memo stands as strong evidence that the company deliberately employs a marketing practice that uses fees to keep up with shareholder obligations to maximize revenue while keeping the published tuition figures artificially low. This allows for-profit colleges to advertise that students are able to cover tuition costs entirely with Title IV funds, even though the additional fees exceed the amount of federal aid a student is eligible for.

These fees, which are separated from tuition for marketing purposes, are most troubling in the sense that they often fail to be disclosed to students until after they have committed to an agreement with the college. In its most basic sense, this is another conventional bait-and-switch tactic. For-profit colleges advertise artificially low tuition rates to students, creating a false sense of financial security that is brought on by an inaccurate understanding of federal aid coverage relative to the real total cost of their education. In order to achieve this, for-profit colleges fail to disclose these additional fees with a series of smoke-and-mirrors techniques. For instance, students at Ashford University, after committing to the institution under the impression that the advertised tuition costs would be the exclusive rate, are charged a "technology fee" of

$1,290 upon the sixth week of enrollment.[19] Additionally, students enrolled in online courses at Westwood College are charged a $40 per-credit-hour fee, which accumulates to more than $6,000 over the duration of a bachelor degree.[20]

In addition to hidden fees, *total* estimated tuition prices are also regularly withheld from students. This method not only helps for-profit colleges to place focus on the supposed benefits from attending the institution and not the cost of the programs, but it also works to further conceal fees and other additional rates. In other words, if prospective students do not know the expected total cost, how could they possibly decipher any hidden fees before committing?

For example, Rasmussen's website features a conspicuous link to the "Tuition" page of the site.[21] Upon clicking the link, entering a zip code, and the degree being pursued, prospective students are brought to a page where the cost per credit hour is revealed but not a *total* tuition estimate.[22] Furthermore, the link also lacks information concerning the number of credit hours that are needed to fulfill the degree requirements, nor does it provide an estimate of annual or term costs of attendance. In many cases, when "tuition" is typed into the search engine, prospective students are introduced to links with pages titled, "Frequently Asked Questions" and "Financial Aid," which often fail to give detailed pricing estimates.[23]

Nonetheless, there are some for-profits that appear to release tuition figures in what seems to be a helpful format. For example, Colorado Technical University, owned and operated by Career Education Corporation, projects a total cost estimate of its "Bachelor's Degree in Business Administration and Management" program at $31,453.[24] Below the estimated tuition projection is a notation that describes additional costs of attendance: "Tuition, Fees & Books information above represents the average total charges incurred by students who completed the program in normal time between 07/01/2009 and 06/30/2010."[25] However, the figures that are disclosed are well out-of-date. Not only has Colorado Technical University failed to update additional fee costs, but it also withholds that, relative to the rates that are disclosed, a student enrolling today could pay nearly $22,000 more over the course of his or her enrollment in future years.[26]

It has been proven that for-profit colleges employ a series of techniques to advertise artificially low tuition rates. This effectively shields prospective students from actual cost projections until they commit to the institution. So what happens when students are eventually assessed the additional fees that make the real costs of attendance significantly higher relative to the rates originally advertised? In most cases, students have received their maximum amount of federal loan and grant eligibility. This, unfortunately, means that additional assistance will not be coming from the government to help the student.

Prior to 2007, the standard alternative of financing was to obtain additional loans through private lending companies. However, following the 2008 credit crash, private lenders have tightened their credit flow, subsequently avoiding entrance as a third-party lender to most for-profit college students.[27] Consequently, many students find themselves out of options. They are eligible for neither additional federal aid nor relief from private lenders.

It is at this point that for-profit colleges offer panicking students what are known as "institutional loans," which are directly provided from the for-profit company to the student. This sets the stage for a particularly favorable playing field for the for-profits. Following changes in the 2008 reauthorization of the Higher Education Act (HEA), these loans are allowed to be considered under the "10" of the earlier noted "90/10 rule."[28] In the words of the CFO at Corinthian Colleges, "Under the current rules we can have these institutional loans count as part of the 10 percent. So, again, we get the benefit of the incremental dollars net of the discount. So if on an ongoing basis 45 percent of that price increase came to us after discount, we get the benefit of that in our 90/10 calculation as part of the 10 percent." As a result, major firms in the for-profit industry have established institutional lending programs, which are funded by a complex set of transactions. In the most basic terms, the loan programs are large sums of money collected and arranged by Wall Street banks. These are then directly channeled to third-party student lenders. From there, the loans are then packaged into securities and sold to investors. In order to promote investment, for-profit firms guarantee the loans by obligating itself to make "recourse" payments to investors if the agreed-upon number of the loans default. Consequently, the Department of Education permits these private loans, which have been generated through a series of transactions, to be counted on the "10" side of the equation.[29]

Before venturing into the repercussions from this growing practice, it is worth examining how for-profit colleges specifically gain access to the funds necessary to operate these institutional lending programs. Because of the incredible complexities surrounding money transfers, there is no single track that is embraced. Therefore, it would be beneficial to examine one of the most effective models in operation today rather than examining a series of corporate pathways.

ITT, which stands as one the most successful for-profit firms in establishing this network of funding mechanisms, provides insight into one of the largest and most efficient models in this regard. The story of ITT's PEAKS program begins with Deutsche Bank, which originally transferred $346 million in loans to ITT students.[30] Borrowing at a 28 percent discounted rate, ITT received $246.7 million in cash from Deutsche Bank.[31] These loans were then sold to a trust, which then issued $300 million in senior debt to Wall Street investors.[32] In accordance to the agreement made between ITT and Deutsche Bank, in exchange for the discounted borrowing rate, ITT was then assessed a subordinated note from the trust. This agreement ultimately "guaranteed the senior debt holders repayment of principal, interest, certain call premiums, and additional administrative fees and expenses, regardless of whether the loans are repaid."[33] In order to ensure a return on this investment, ITT charges a variable interest rate to borrowing students, ranging from 4.75 to 14.75 percent.[34]

The case of ITT is but one of countless for-profit institutions that have chosen to embrace institutional loans. For example, Corinthian Colleges, Inc., lent $65 million in institutional loans to students in the fiscal year of 2009 alone, with an average interest rate of 14.8 percent.[35] While the interest rate on federal Stafford loans made by the Department of Education equated to 3.4 percent during the same year, other leading for-profits surpassed that figure by roughly fivefold. Further cases demonstrate that, while Education Management Corporation capped its interest rates at 11.2 percent, Alta Colleges, Inc., led the industry in charging interest rates as high as 18 percent.[36] Between these two extreme institutional interest rates were DeVry, Inc., at 12 percent; Career Education Corporation at 13 percent; and Kaplan Higher Education, Inc., at 15 percent.[37]

However, the most startling component of this web of transactions is not the absent safeguards to debtors nor the excessive industry-wide interest rates. The most concerning aspect of this elaborate scheme is the fact that for-profits expect large numbers of their students to default on these institutional loans but continue to offer them anyway. As a senior Kaplan executive emphasized in an internal memo, "we should assume an 80% default rate for loans in repayment."[38] Later detail reveals that these estimates were based on private student loans made by a private lender to Kaplan students, which had "experienced defaults of 70 percent and 65 percent for loans made in 2006 and 2007, respectively."[39]

Although this appalling estimate of 80 percent stands out as the industry's clear leader, similar memos from other for-profits reveal that Kaplan is not alone in their predictions. Compared to an expected default rate of 16 percent on federally issued student loans from the Department of Education, Education Management Corporation estimated a 42 percent default rate, while Career Education Corporation had similar projections at 48 percent, and Corinthian Colleges, Inc., at 55 percent.[40]

As earlier noted, most students who are involved in institutional lending programs have been driven to them as a result of already having exhausted their federal aid eligibility. These assessments account for the likely risk of default as a result of the circumstances. Consequently, although the for-profit education sector only accounts for 12 percent of total college enrollment, the industry is responsible for 47 percent of the total amount of student loan defaults nationwide.[41]

Compared to the 13 percent of community college students who take out loans to pay for their degrees, as well as the 48 percent of students at four-year public colleges and the 57 percent at four-year private not-for-profit colleges, 96 percent of students enrolled in the for-profit industry require loans in order to pay for college (see figure 6.3).[42] This point alone illustrates the financial pressure uniquely placed on students in the for-profit market. Over time, for-profit executives have examined that there is a correlative relationship between tuition rates and withdrawal rates. This is evident in that, as tuition rises, so do the number of withdrawals.

Consistent with this trend, a director of admissions for Herzing's Madison campus stressed the significant burden of increased debt and default on students in a 2009 e-mail to corporate executives: "We would prefer to see no increases as there is already a struggle for many stu-

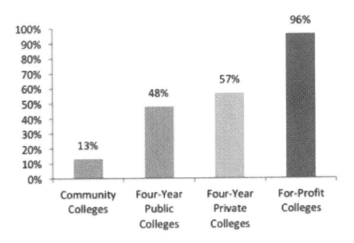

Figure 6.3.   Share of Student Borrowing by Sector. *For Profit Higher Education: The Failure to Safeguard the Federal Investment and Ensure Student Success*, Figure: Share of Students Borrowing by Sector, 112.

dents. . . . . Any increase will make it much more difficult for students to be able to graduate in their programs. This is only adding to the student's debt without them gaining additional marketable skills/degrees."[43] Additionally, a director of financial services at Herzing added, "In my experience, and especially lately, the majority of our students cannot afford higher payments. . . . I'm concerned that we will have increased drops and fewer starts."[44] Despite these pleas, the company disregarded this memo and increased tuition by more than 5 percent.[45]

Similar to this conversation at Herzing, Kaplan executives also discussed the potential consequences of increased borrowing levels as a result of higher tuition: "Increases above 3 percent . . . would cause a disruption in student packaging expectations that would lead students to reduce their class loads, or as worst case scenario, drop from our programs to attend a cheaper program where they could reduce out-of-pocket tuition expenses."[46]

Likewise, an Apollo official reported an "increase in the reason that the student is not returning to school is because they are advising that the price increase/high tuition is preventing them from returning."[47] It is fairly evident that for-profit administrators are aware of the effect that higher tuition has in raising withdrawal rates. Unfortunately, the data reveals that these claims are likely correct.

Statistics show that among the nation's worst offenders, 69 percent of students who began at a for-profit college in the 2008–2009 school year left without a degree within a median of 124 days after admission (see figure 6.4).[48] This means that almost 600,000 students left for-profit colleges without a degree in 2010 alone. Further examination reveals a breakdown of withdrawals within each type of program. While 62.9 percent of students in associate degree programs, roughly 300,000 students, withdrew from college, 54.3 percent, approximately 200,000 students, withdrew from bachelor degree programs and 38.5 percent, or 100,000 students, withdrew from certificate programs.[49]

Unfortunately, investigations into the for-profit sector also reveal that the worst offenders in this regard also happen to be some of the largest companies in the industry. For instance, Bridgepoint Education, Inc., leads associate degree withdrawal rates in the for-profit industry at an 84 percent withdrawal rate.[50] Comparably, Kaplan Higher Education, Inc., holds a 69 percent withdrawal rate for associate degree programs, resulting in more than 23,000 students leaving in 2010 before earning a degree.[51]

Arguably the most disturbing single figure in this category is that of Apollo Group, Inc., which singlehandedly failed almost 118,000 students, or 66 percent of their associate degree enrollment, who eventually withdrew in 2010.[52] Hypothetically, if each of these 596,155 with-

Company	Schools Operated	Withdrawn
Bridgepoint	Ashford University	84%
Lincoln	LTI, Euphoria Institute	70%
Wash. Post	Kaplan University	69%
Corinthian	Everest College	66%
Apollo	University of Phoenix	66%
Keiser	Keiser University	65%
EDMC	Brown Mackie College	64%
Average Withdrawal Rate		69.1%

Figure 6.4.   Highest Withdrawal Rates for Associate's Degree Students Enrolling in 2008–2009. *For Profit Higher Education: The Failure to Safeguard the Federal Investment and Ensure Student Success,* Figure: For Profit Companies With Highest Associate Degree Withdrawal Rates, 74.

drawn students were eligible for the full $13,205 in federal student aid, taxpayers lost approximately $7.9 billion on a failed four-month investment in 2010 alone. Following this analysis, we must ask ourselves, Is this an investment worthy of students or taxpayers?

ESSENTIAL TAKEAWAYS

From internal memos, the testimonies of former students, and released company projections, we begin to understand what enrolled students face at this stage of their college experience. For-profit companies strategically misrepresent the estimated cost of college to students in order to gain their financial commitment. Having made this commitment to the for-profit college under false pretenses, students are often assessed additional fees that are hidden in piles of fine print. In most cases, these students have already depleted their federal grant and loan eligibility in order to pay for what was advertised as the original "tuition."

With these hidden fees now due, federal student aid exhausted, and the inability to independently qualify for a private loan large enough to cover the remaining costs, students are out of options. The only remaining choice is to accept an institutional loan with exorbitant interest rates, which is often circumstantially impossible to pay off.

Over time, the price to attend college becomes so burdensome that many students have only the option to cut their losses and withdraw. Before the student even picks up the phone to an initial recruitment call, for-profit education companies know that failure and financial disaster ultimately awaits an overwhelming majority of their student prospects. If this does not qualify as predatory lending, I cannot possibly fathom what does.

7

DREAMS DESTROYED

In response to rising default rates, Congress amended the Higher Education Act in 2008, providing that in 2014 "colleges will be required to demonstrate that no more than 30 percent of students default on Federal student loans within 3 years of entering repayment on their loans."[1] Hoping to comply with this new 30 percent cap, for-profit companies worked quickly to ensure that they did not lose federal aid eligibility, keeping in mind that federal tax dollars account for funding 86 percent of the industry.

One of the market's worst offenders in this regard, Corinthian Colleges, Inc., operated seventy-eight institutions with default rates above 30 percent prior to the new HEA provisions in 2008, before closing its doors in the spring of 2015.[2] "Among all the students leaving Corinthian-owned schools from 2005–8, over 73,000 defaulted," climbing to a pinnacle of 36.1 percent in 2008.[3] However, with the new 2014 standard in place, Corinthian reported that it had reduced the number of defaults by more than half, ending the 2009 projections at thirty-two institutions.[4] Subsequently, Corinthian reported that it was able to lower its total default rate to 28.8 percent, a decrease of 7.3 percent from its 2008 rate, avoiding the 30 percent ceiling by just 1.2 percent.[5] Despite these efforts, "for-profit institutions [still] had the highest average three-year default rate at 22.7 percent, with public institutions following at 11 percent and private non-profit institutions at 7.5 percent."[6]

At first glance, it appears that the for-profit industry is beginning to take real action in supporting students with adequate financial management assistance. This assumption, however, would be incorrect. Closer examination reveals that former students of for-profit colleges are actually in greater debt than they were before the 2008 adjustments and the subsequent market maneuvers thereafter. If for-profit firms have lowered the three-year default rate, what can possibly explain this outcome?

To put it simply, in response to the three-year default standard, many for-profit schools have allocated resources to mechanisms that exempt students from default for the duration of the three-year monitoring window. To do so, for-profit colleges have launched an aggressive campaign to apply forbearance and deferment to students in order to temporarily delay repayments long enough to avoid the new standard. Ideally, students are able to repay their student loans with a repayment plan upon employment, which is split into monthly payments. However, when the student falls behind in repayment, it is easier for these colleges to transfer the student into deferment or forbearance for the three-year monitoring window. Rather than taking the risk of adjusting the repayment plan only for the student to fall behind again and default, this ensures that college default rates remain artificially below the three-year 30 percent threshold.

Before examining the effects of these decisions, it is important to know exactly what terms like *deferment* or *forbearance* mean. "A deferment is a period during which repayment of the principal (the total sum of money borrowed plus any interest that has been capitalized/interest that has been added to the principal balance) and interest of the loan is temporarily delayed."[7] Whereas, forbearance is a period during which the borrower continues to pay off the principal but is temporarily relieved of the interest payments. However, additional interest still accrues on the interest that is not paid off each month, leading to an end result of compounding interest. The compounding interest, over the course of this three-year window, eventually adds up to thousands of dollars in additional debt that could have otherwise been avoided had the student been permitted to simply readjust the repayment plan.

Pauline Abernathy, vice president of the Institute for College Access and Success, speaks to this problem in her testimony to the Senate HELP Committee in a June 2011 hearing: "Putting students willy-nilly into forbearance when it is not in their interest to be in forbearance just increases the likelihood of default. These students still face a high risk of default, but on a higher balance. Thus, this delaying tactic may help a school while harming students."[8] Simply put, when there is a conflict of interests between what is best for the student and what is favorable to the firm, the firm is willing to sacrifice the long-term security of the student's future in order to ensure that its federal aid eligibility status remains intact. With the definitions of *deferment* and *forbearance* established, let us turn to how a majority of students are directed into these avenues of unnecessary long-term debt.

As default has become increasingly difficult to manage by the for-profit colleges themselves, many companies have resorted to hiring third-party default management vendors. At least twelve of the thirty companies under investigation contract with the largest of these firms, General Revenue Corporation (GRC), a subsidiary of Sallie Mae.[9] Deploying a network of call centers, GRC advises delinquent students on possible ways to "cure" their default. Although GRC claims to explain to students "all repayment options, including income-based repayment plans," internal documents from the largest for-profit education companies prove otherwise.[10]

Figures from 2009 exhibit that, of the student profiles that were managed by GRC, an average of 76 percent were forbearances or deferments, while only 24 percent were repayments.[11] As the 2014 standard and its penalties for colleges who fail to stay below the three-year 30 percent threshold drew closer, internal GRC documents demonstrate that there has been an even greater shift away from repayment. Between 2009 and 2010, there was a drop of nearly 7 percent in student repayment profiles, from 24.6 percent in 2009 down to 18 percent in 2010.[12] This 7 percent of students were simply transferred from repayment plans to deferment, which rose to 30.5 percent in 2010, up from 23.4 percent in 2009.[13]

The financial agreements between for-profit firms and third-party default management vendors stand as one possible explanation for this model of transferring thousands of students into deferment or forbearance, along with the additional economic strains that come with it in the long run. Many companies, like Corinthian and ITT, pay large bonuses for "cures" that exceed their baseline demands, regardless of the type. "This bonus can be as much as $120 per cure, on top of the standard fee of $30 to $40 for each student account placed with the company."[14]

Operating in this atmosphere, third-party vendors often have no financial incentive to consider the student's long-term debt or financial security. The primary focus is making sure that students do not default during the three-year monitoring window. Once the three years are up and the student ceases to be counted toward the examined default figures, that account is no longer a priority. A Remington executive confirms this, stating, "We've known all along what ED finally figured out—that most of the borrowers who receive payment postponements (forbearance, deferment) during the cohort period, ultimately default after postponement ends."[15]

Aside from third-party default managers becoming increasingly involved in this process, for-profit colleges still run their own default management campaigns in order to reduce default figures. Corinthian Colleges, Inc., which owned and operated Everest, Wyotech, and Heald Colleges, has been historically among the worst default rates in all of higher education. Of the 65,485 Corinthian students who began repayment on their loans in 2008, 12,671 defaulted within two years, while another 23,623 defaulted within three years.[16] In response to these incredibly high figures, California stripped all fourteen of Corinthian's Everest campuses, as well as two Wyotech and two Heald campuses, of their state aid eligibility status for student grant programs.[17]

In order to avoid a similar response from the federal government once the 2014 penalties became enforceable, Corinthian allocated considerable resources to reduce the company's reported default rate. Their plan was simple: Drive students at risk of defaulting into forbearance by any means necessary. Executives told investors in May 2011, "Forbearance, as you know, is a pretty easy solution, just a question you have to agree to and you're on your way."[18] Highlighting that, although the company had seen drastic improvements in their default numbers, "Our repayment rate really has not moved a whole heck of a lot from where it was prior to this effort."[19] This essentially means that while the company benefits from an artificially low default rate, thousands of Corinthian students continue to sink deeper into abysmal levels of debt without any help from the college whatsoever.

Corinthian's primary method of reducing default rates was to hire three major default management contractors, one being GRC, which devoted sixty full-time employees to make between 2 and 2.5 million calls a year to former Corinthian students. That is an average of 102 calls per employee on every day of the year.[20] Additionally, Corinthian also constructed its own network of internal default management mechanisms primarily based around a central call center that housed dozens of its own employees.[21]

Echoing the same language of recruitment manuals, default management employees are instructed to engage in similar high-pressure sales tactics to "close the sale."[22] This practice was taken to new levels of indignity during a February 2010 campaign, which offered gift cards to McDonald's for students who contacted the default management department and signed off on forbearance or deferment if their repayment plan at the time was not viable.[23] This seems to bring the theme of the for-profits to full circle. High-pressure sales tactics and gimmicks are used right from the very beginning, during the recruitment stage, all the way through to even after the student has left in order to squeeze every last cent from their pockets.

For students who do fall victim to "close the sale" techniques, how much additional debt are they incurring? Data shows that a student who enters forbearance for thirty-six months will end up paying about 30 percent more over the life of their loan.[24] For instance, the average Vatterott student leaves school with roughly $11,000 in debt. Figures from the Department of Education reveal that these students, if convinced to enter into forbearance, will end up owing $3,100 in addition to the $11,000 principal over the course of the next ten years.[25] Similarly, a graduate from Chancellor who originally bears an average $18,267 in principal debt, ends up paying an additional $5,146 following a three-year forbearance period.[26]

However, these are small amounts relative to what students at many of the largest for-profit colleges face. Former Kaplan student Eric Schmitt, for example, described his student loan repayment problems to the Senate HELP Committee in his testimony on June 7, 2011:

> I owe $45,000 in student loans without a permanent job to pay those bills. Only very rarely in the past seven years since completing my associates have I been able to make any payments at all, and the debt continues to pile up. The loans from my associate degree went in default late last year. The loans from my bachelor's degree are in deferment, but I have no idea how I will manage after my deferment time runs out. Because of the deferment and forbearances, the inter-

est has added more than 10 percent on top of my original balance, and in this battle, it seems even time is against me.[27]

Remember, this is the same Eric Schmitt who invested this life-altering sum of money for a nonaccredited paralegal studies program at Kaplan.[28] In addition to the principal sum, Schmitt will likely struggle for the rest of his life to pay off the 10 percent interest that Kaplan knowingly passed on when they encouraged him to agree to a forbearance period. Consequently, students are often harmed more than they are helped in the long term due to the additional costs associated with deferment and forbearance.

Thus far, everything we have discussed has been focused on a short window of time, including recruitment, attendance, and the three-year monitoring period following loan repayment initiation. This last portion of this analysis is meant to consider some of the long-term implications that arise as a consequence of this deeply flawed and fundamentally backward system of for-profit higher education.

The first concern when addressing such long-term repercussions is the average cost to for-profit students relative to students in other sectors. Financially independent students, a population that makes up a majority of for-profit enrollment, left the for-profit industry with a median debt of $32,700 in 2008,[29] whereas independent students at private nonprofit colleges departed with a median debt of $24,600, while those at public colleges acquired a total median debt of $20,000.[30] This translates to private colleges being, on average, 25 percent cheaper than a for-profit education and public schools offering a staggering 39 percent cheaper rate than their for-profit counterparts. While many students enrolled in for-profit bachelor degree programs do not graduate, many of the 57 percent who do owe sums of $30,000 or more.[31] Conversely, only 25 percent of graduates in the private nonprofit sector and 12 percent from the public sector were obligated to borrow that amount at the time.[32] From a financial perspective alone, it is clear that students in the for-profit realm are immediately placed at a disadvantage compared to students in other sectors, aside from the debate on the market worth of for-profit programs.

For instance, ITT reports that a bachelor of business administration, after factoring in tuition, fees, interest, and so on, costs an estimated $93,624 in 2011.[33] This means that a student who qualified for the maximum amount of Pell grants and federal Stafford loans was still unable to pay for an ITT bachelor degree. Granted, this is an extremely high rate relative to the median cost of comparable degrees in the industry, which hold an average estimated cost that is roughly 30 percent less than the ITT business administration program.[34]

Nonetheless, a comparable degree from the public sector, like SUNY Buffalo, amounted to a four-year total of $19,880 that same year.[35] This comes to a savings of 79 percent over the course of a four-year program. As for associate degree programs, ITT charges $48,228 for an associate in business administration, while Corinthian-owned Everest College charged $43,344 for the same degree.[36] Some of the lower for-profit market rates for an associate in business administration can be found at Kaplan University, which charges $30,065, and the University of Phoenix at $24,000.[37]

However, even the cheapest for-profit associate's degree programs are exponentially higher than two-year public alternatives. Community colleges across the country held an average total tuition price of $5,926 in 2011.[38] This means that a student who invests in an associate degree from a community college can save from 75 to 88 percent, depending on which side of the for-profit associate degree price spectrum is being examined.

Regardless of whether a student withdraws or graduates, these high debt loads place an unnecessarily high financial burden on students after leaving the for-profit industry. The debt is often so insurmountable that students will spend the rest of their lives trying to recover. One complaint from a Lincoln student appropriately articulates this crisis: "I went to school to better my life, and when my loans become due, I will actually be in worse financial shape than I was before I attended school. I wish I would have never attended school at all."[39] An ITT student aimed his criticism at the high cost of his program as well, commenting, "I've heard of 10k for a 2 year degree, but 40k?"[40] However, another ITT student captures this scenario better than anyone else: "I took out student loans in the hopes of improving my knowledge so that I could improve my worth in society, for a higher paying job. Instead, now I have a loan to pay off and absolutely nothing to show for it."[41]

As a consequence of students incurring large levels of debt "with nothing to show for it," the Department of Education estimates that

46.3 percent of all dollars lent to for-profit students who entered repayment in 2008 will eventually default over the course of the debtor's lifetime.[42]

In 2008, there were 1,115,097 students enrolled in the for-profit sector.[43] Hypothetically, if we came to the conclusion that every single person on average received the same amount of loans, it would mean that everyone also had an equal share of possible default. Under this reasoning, 46.3 percent of the 1,115,097 students enrolled in 2008 will eventually default over the course of their lifetimes. This would mean that from a single enrollment year, 516,290 people would eventually become so financially desperate that they would have no alternative other than to default. Realize that this number is from a single year. Over the course of a decade, that is almost 5.2 million people who will face that same fate.

The status quo is unstainable. Each year, more than a million students enrolled in the for-profit higher-education sector unknowingly sign away any hope of future success. This cannot continue. The economic burden of financing the for-profit industry is as unacceptable to taxpayers as it is inhumane to the individuals who are duped into accruing a lifetime of debt for nothing. There is a system in place that provides little to no return to the consumer, for both taxpayers and individual students alike.

In what other market does this phenomenon take place? If we go to a grocery store, we expect that bread and milk will not be sold past its expiration date. If we go to a mechanic, we assume that the repairs will make the car safer and more able to function properly. Why should higher education be any different? A for-profit parallel to the grocery store analogy would be like going to the store, being overcharged for expired milk, and then not having the right to return it for a refund.

Instead of inviting thought and innovation by means of adequate programs, for-profits falsely sell overpriced services for a degree that will be useless to a majority of its students. The for-profit industry is a fleet of used-car salesmen with a lot full of lemons. They know that their product is substandard and their price is too high, but they sell it to you for a premium anyway with promises that cannot be kept. For all of these reasons, this crisis demands a strong and immediate reaction from lawmakers.

ESSENTIAL TAKEAWAYS

In an attempt to avoid harsh penalties for high default rates across the sector, for-profit colleges have systematically transferred students from repayment to deferment and forbearance as a way to deliberately manipulate default rates. Employing and working alongside third-party default management vendors, for-profit higher education companies engage in an unprecedented level of predatory college lending. Fully aware of the fact that such actions will financially cripple many of its students for the rest of their lives, for-profit colleges come full circle in their practices. Deceiving their students at every level of their education, from recruiting to lending, for-profit colleges have buried millions of students with vast sums of debt and compounding interest with virtually nothing to show for it.

8

CONGRESSIONAL CONSPIRACY

Considering the discussion of the for-profit industry, surrounding both its practices and its funding, one would assume that finding a solution would be a top priority in Congress. Unfortunately, that is not the case. Aside from consumer protection mavericks, such as Senator Tom Harkin, Senator Dick Durbin, Senator Jack Reed, and Senator Elizabeth Warren, Congress has been surprisingly silent on this issue.

The root of this congressional inaction can be found in the enormous profit margins of the industry. These are led by ITT Educational Services, Inc., which had a 37.1 percent profit margin in 2009, followed by Strayer Education, Inc., at 33.7 percent; Apollo Group, Inc. at 27 percent; and American Public Education, Inc., at 26.8 percent.[1] Of the thirty companies investigated by the Senate HELP Committee, twenty-four posted double-digit profit margins. Although Apollo Group, Inc., had only the third-highest percentage rate in 2009, it posted the largest financial profit at $1.1 billion that same year.[2] Additionally, Apollo Group received $3.1 billion in federal student aid, as well as $46 million in military education benefits.[3] This combined sum effectively represents 86.8 percent of the firm's revenue, and approximately $925 million of that was accounted as direct profit.[4] Bear in mind, this extraordinary investment helped to finance a company that led more than 118,000 of its students to withdraw in 2010.[5]

Despite the significant amount of federal revenue that is directed toward a failing investment, for-profit firms continue to sustain their large share of taxpayer revenue. However, the institutions themselves are not the exclusive beneficiaries because many of their executives receive substantial compensation. As millions are driven into default, these executives earn fortunes in the millions, and sometimes tens of millions, of dollars.

For example, two Strayer Education, Inc., executives are among the highest paid in the for-profit realm. While the president and CEO earned a base salary, bonuses, and stock options that amounted to $10,839,800 in 2009, Strayer's chairman and CEO led the industry at $41,489,800 the same year.[6] However, they are not alone. Other notables include Apollo Group's chairman and CEO, who made $8,617,597 in 2009, as well as Bridgepoint's chairman and CEO, who was paid $20,532,304 over the same fiscal year.[7] Although Bridgepoint's chairman and CEO only came in second place on the 2009 salary standings list, he still managed to hold first place as the industry's overseer of the highest associate degree withdrawal rate of 84 percent.[8] Clearly, he is not being compensated enough for his efforts.

In contrast to these sums, chief administrators from nonprofit higher-educational sectors make a fraction of these eight-figure for-profit paychecks. For instance, Harvard University is often considered to be one of the best higher-education institutions in the world. Compared to the immense levels of for-profit compensation in 2009, Harvard's president was paid a total of $822,000,[9] while the average salary of college presidents at the top eight Ivy League schools was $1.1 million that same year.[10]

Understanding that these cases are limited to only an extreme few, our focus next turns to executive pay that is more reflective of the greater higher-education market. While median compensation to the five highest-paid for-profit executives totaled $16,192,230, and the median salary to the five highest-paid public college executives was $1,027,820; the median of comparable executives in the nonprofit private sector was $3,044,520.[11] This is especially troubling because, as the Senate HELP Committee report concluded, there is an increasing disconnect between the profit of education companies and the value for students. "Revenues [from federal financial aid dollars] continue to grow even though most students leave without completing a degree, and many are not able to make payments on their student loan debt."[12]

Aside from the debate on what should determine executive salaries in different sectors of higher education, there is one fact that is indisputable. The profits accumulated by for-profit firms have led to a substantial lobbying campaign in recent years that is meant to suppress meaningful reform. Before illustrating the magnitude of this recent upsurge in lobbying, let us examine why the for-profit industry has taken this initiative.

With the issuance of highly critical government reports, 2010 was a bad year for the for-profit sector. Following several years of data collection, testimony, and review of internal documents, the US Senate HELP Committee and the Government Accountability Office (GAO) unleashed an unrelenting referendum on the for-profit industry. On June 24, 2010, the Senate HELP Committee issued "Emerging Risk?: An Overview of Growth, Spending, Student Debt and Unanswered Questions in For-Profit Higher Education," which established both the rising debt loads of students as well as the rapid increase in tax dollars that are used to fund the industry. These figures were then compared to the record profit margins and executive salaries in the industry. Roughly six weeks later, the GAO published its "For-Profit Colleges: Undercover Testing Finds Colleges Encouraged Fraud and Engaged in Deceptive and Questionable Marketing Practices" on August 2, 2010. This report worked to enhance the understanding of the misleading and fraudulent recruitment practices of the industry after undercover GAO officials posed as prospective students. Examples of this range from students being encouraged to "falsify their financial aid forms to qualify for federal aid" and "pressuring applicants to sign a contract for enrollment before allowing them to speak to a financial advisor about program costs and financing options."[13]

Less than two months later, the Senate HELP Committee ramped up its rhetoric, filing a report called "The Return of the Federal Investment in For-Profit Education: Debt without a Diploma." The findings of this report built on the point of the industry's rising dependence on federal aid and concentrated on the astonishing withdrawal rates at for-profit firms.

The Senate HELP Committee ended its 2010 referendum of for-profit schools with its report "Benefiting Whom? For-Profit Education Companies and the Growth of Military Education Benefits" on December 8, 2010. This methodically explained the industry's particular attention to military veterans and their eligibility for financial education benefits, as well as the marketing schemes that are deployed to capture these additional funds. Over this six-month period, the Senate HELP Committee and the GAO systematically undermined the image of the for-profit market, calling for an immediate legislative response.

Simultaneously, President Obama indicated his own scrutiny of the industry. As Nick Anderson of the *Washington Post* wrote, under the president's "'gainful employment' rule, programs at for-profit schools . . . would be held accountable for how much debt their graduates accumulate relative to annual income and for whether former students are repaying the principal on their loans."[14] In a less direct affront to for-profit colleges, President Obama also spoke at several college campuses during the time these Senate reports were released, telling students at the University of Texas in Austin that community colleges are an "under-appreciated asset that we should value and support."[15] The promotion of community colleges is particularly frightening to for-profit firms because community colleges are arguably the largest immediate competitor to the for-profit industry.

In a countermaneuver, the industry responded with an approximate 250 percent hike in lobbying and campaign contribution expenditures over a single year, climbing to $8.1 million in donations to congressional members in 2010.[16] This amount continued to increase in the following years, as for-profit firms spent $8.1 million in the first nine months of 2011 alone.[17] Of the roughly $16 million spent during this twenty-one-month period, $11.9 million can be traced back to the largest companies in the for-profit industry that collectively financed 158 lobbyists at 37 separate firms.[18] Individual firm contributions to this effort range from $1.6 million in contributions from Career Education Corporation to the $1.2 million payment from Bridgepoint Education, Inc. (see figure 8.1).[19]

In addition to the sheer amount of money that was contributed in lobbying efforts and campaign contributions, we should consider who the primary beneficiaries of these funds are and how these particular recipients are uniquely situated in Congress to have an effect on higher-education policy.

Although lobbyists have access to budgets spanning into the millions of dollars, there is still a limited number of resources that can be allocated to members of Congress. Subsequently, lobbying firms target individuals in Congress who will provide the highest return on their

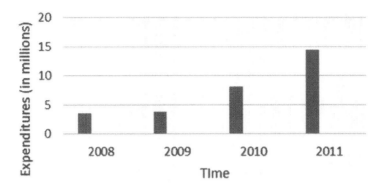

Figure 8.1.   For-Profit Lobbying Trends. *For Profit Higher Education: The Failure to Safeguard the Federal Investment and Ensure Student Success,* **85.**

investment. What does this mean? Senior members of Congress with high levels of authority are the ones who are sought after in this regard.

There are several factors that explain why this occurs; most notably is the issue of seniority. Particularly prevalent in the House of Representatives, hierarchical party influence works to compel freshman members of Congress to vote the way party leadership wishes them to:

> Congressional seniority is one example of a system in which institutional age (as opposed to chronological age or experience) is relevant to the behavior of individual actors. . . . The seniority system in the U.S. House of Representatives is a collection of formal and informal rules and norms through which long-serving members control more resources than do their more junior colleagues.[20]

In other words, the longer a person is in Congress, the higher likelihood that person holds a high level of authority and influence in the chamber based on the significance of their committee assignment. From their positions of party authority, these members have influence over behavior throughout the chamber because young members who wish to eventually reach these prominent positions must demonstrate party loyalty.

Models of the relationship between party loyalty and committee assignments "indicate that loyalty to the party leadership is a statistically and substantively important determinant of who gets what assignment."[21] Therefore, a majority of new members are restricted as independent actors by their compliance with demands from party leadership in respect to voting behavior. Hence, party leadership not only holds the most influential committee assignments, but they can also have a broad impact on voting behavior throughout the entire chamber.

In addition to the influence that seniority has on voting behavior throughout the chamber, lobbyists must also place a particular focus on members who are assigned to committees with jurisdiction over bills that are relevant to their specific interests. Shifting from party influence to the procedural powers of specific committees, lobbying and campaign contributions tend to focus on two types of relevant committees.

The first category can be classified as "prestige committees," which hold "tremendous" procedural power over the chamber.[22] These three committees include the House Committee on Rules, which sets the political agenda by determining special procedural exemptions to fast-track a bill to the House floor; the House Committee on Ways and Means, which handles any matters concerning taxes or revenues; and the House Committee on Appropriations, which determines how money is distributed. It becomes clear why an influence over the House Committee on Rules would be particularly important in terms of guaranteeing preferential treatment toward your specific interest when the agenda is being set.

Aside from the three prestige committees, the House has more than a dozen "policy or constituency committees."[23] As highly specialized bodies that handle specific issues, ranging from agriculture to veterans' affairs, these committees receive and review any bills that are relevant to their jurisdiction after they have been introduced on the floor of the chamber.[24] During this phase of the legislative process, the bill faces the obstacle of surviving the "political agenda of the majority party and the committee chair, as well as the committee's rules."[25] For the few bills that make it past these challenges, a series of hearings are often conducted to collect additional information. From there,

> The committee chair can refer the bill to one or more subcommittees based on their jurisdictions as listed in the committee rules, or the chair can hold the bill at the full committee level and not refer it to a subcommittee. Holding the bill at full committee level means one of two things: either the bill will be acted on quickly or it is being suppressed and will die from neglect.[26]
>
> Therefore, whoever controls the committee controls the fate of any relevant bills. Statistics from the 110th Congress reveal exactly

how crucial this committee phase of a bill actually is. Of the 11,056 bills that were introduced and referred to committees for review, 9,904 died while in committee and had no chance of ever being voted on as a consequence.[27] This means that committees killed 89.6 percent of the bills they received during the 110th Congress alone. Therefore, it is absolutely necessary to have an influence on the committees with relevant jurisdiction if one is to ensure their interests. In the House, any bill that concerns education is referred to the House Committee on Education and the Workforce. Thus, for-profit lobbying firms direct most of their attention to the members on this committee.

Although the House Committee on Education and the Workforce is a body of forty-one members, twenty-three Republicans and eighteen Democrats, three people stand out as the most important individuals on this particular committee.[28] The most significant of the three is the committee chair, which has been occupied by John Kline, a Republican from Minnesota's second district, since 2010. The committee chair enjoys certain exclusive powers in that he or she not only leads any discussion or hearings that are conducted by the full committee, but the chair also has the power to either delegate the bill to a subcommittee or smother it by holding the bill until it dies. In order to gauge how the for-profit higher-education industry has attempted to influence Rep. Kline, we must turn to recent campaign financing figures that reveal contributions both before and after his appointment as chair to the House Committee on Education and the Workforce.

To do so, our examination begins with the 2007–2008 fund-raising cycle, which was the last campaign that Kline ran before being appointed as committee chair. During this time, not one of Rep. Kline's top twenty donors came from the education sector, nor was the for-profit higher-education sector as a whole listed as one of the top twenty contributing industries.[29] However, following his appointment as chair to the House Committee on Education and the Workforce in 2010, Kline received a vastly different level of contributions from the education sector during the 2011–2012 fund-raising cycle. During his first campaign as committee chairman, the education sector led as Kline's top contributing industry, providing a total $269,559 to his campaign.[30] Additionally, the list of his top donors from this same cycle reveals a significant initiative from several individual for-profit firms as well.

With for-profit education companies listed as three of his top four do-nors,[31] Apollo Group led as the highest single contributor, paying Kline's campaign $21,500.[32] Other for-profit education companies fol-lowed close behind, like Rasmussen, Inc., at $16,419 and DeVry, Inc., at $16,250.[33]

However, these firms were not alone, as other companies, including Education Management Corp., the Association of Private Sector Col-leges/Universities, Capella Education, and Herzing College, were all notable top-twenty patrons to the John Kline campaign in 2012.[34] As indicated by the amount of funds pouring in from for-profit higher-education companies during his time as chairman, the statistics sur-rounding Rep. Kline irrefutably highlight the incredible value of the chair position, as well as the industry's serious commitment to ensuring favorable treatment from whomever occupies its seat.

Within the House Committee on Education and the Workforce, there are four subcommittees. These include the House Subcommittee on Early Childhood, Elementary, and Secondary Education; the House Subcommittee on Health, Employment, Labor, and Pensions; the House Subcommittee on Higher Education and Workforce Training; and the House Subcommittee on Workforce Protections.[35] The sub-committee most relevant to for-profit higher education is the House Subcommittee on Higher Education and Workforce Training. The chairwoman of this subcommittee is Virginia Foxx, a Republican repre-senting North Carolina's fifth district.[36] This position is among one of the most important positions on the House Committee on Education and the Workforce because if a bill concerning higher education is passed down from the committee chair, it is certain that it will be deferred to this subcommittee.

Although Rep. Kline still receives the highest level of financial sup-port from the for-profit education sector, contributions in recent years to Rep. Foxx have still been significant. During the 2011–2012 fund-raising cycle, Foxx received $62,068 from education lobbying firms, standing as the second-highest contributing industry to Foxx during this period.[37] As for specific donors, for-profit higher-education lobbying firms stood as two of the top three individual contributors to her cam-paign: the Association of Private Sector Colleges/Universities at $10,000 and Warburg Pincus at $9,000.[38] Other notables on this list include ECPI College of Technology based out of Virginia as well as Keiser

University, both at $5,500.[39] Following this steady flow of campaign funds to Rep. Foxx during this cycle, firms in the for-profit industry can reasonably hope for favorable treatment during future bill consideration and markup from the House Subcommittee on Higher Education and Workforce Training.

Aside from Rep. John Kline and Rep. Virginia Foxx, arguably the two most powerful figures in the House of Representatives in regard to bills concerning higher education, there is one final seasoned member of the House who should be recognized as a significant beneficiary of contributions from the for-profit education sector. Howard "Buck" McKeon has been representing California's twenty-fifth district in the House since 1993. McKeon stands as a senior member of the House Committee on Education and the Workforce, having been the committee chair between 2006 and 2007 before being replaced by Democrat George Miller in 2008.

During this lengthy career in the House, Rep. McKeon has been the beneficiary of several for-profit lobbying firms and relevant companies from the for-profit higher-education sector. The leader in this regard is SLM Corp., which owns and operates Sallie Mae as well as its subsidiary General Revenue Corporation.[40] Over the course of his career in the House, Rep. McKeon has received $86,250 from SLM Corp. as well as $64,000 from Apollo Group and $58,308 from the Association of Private Sector Colleges/Universities.[41] When the topic of seniority influence in the House is factored into this equation of whom to invest in as a lobbying firm, there is no other member more valuable to for-profit firms than Rep. McKeon.

Although the funding provided to these three powerful members of the House Committee on Education and the Workforce increases the likelihood of favorable legislative outcomes, lobbying firms take additional measures to ensure their objective of influencing policy. According to "Rule 11: Quorums" of the official rules of the committee,

> One-third of the members of the Committee or subcommittee shall constitute a quorum for taking any action other than amending Committee rules, closing a meeting from the public, reporting a measure or recommendation, or in the case of the Committee or a subcommittee authorizing a subpoena. For the enumerated actions, a majority of the Committee or subcommittee shall constitute a quorum.

> Any two members shall constitute a quorum for the purpose of taking testimony and receiving evidence.[42]

As a result, for-profit lobbying firms must guarantee the support of fourteen of the forty-one committee members in order to be absolutely certain of safeguarding their interests. To no surprise, the for-profit sector was listed as a top-twenty donor industry to eleven additional members in the 2011–2012 cycle, including:[43]

David Loebsack (D), IA-2
Carolyn McCarthy (D), NY-4
Robert Andrews (D), NJ-1
Jared Polis (D), CO-2
George Miller (D), CA-11
Robert Scott (D), VA-3
Timothy Bishop (D), NY-1
Thomas Petri (R), WI-6
Trey Gowdy (R), SC-4
Glenn Thompson (R), PA-5
Lou Barletta (R), PA-11

Although they are not the sole beneficiaries of for-profit education lobbying efforts, these eleven additional members, when combined with Kline, Foxx, and McKeon, reach the fourteen-person threshold for a successful quorum on the House Committee on Education and the Workforce.

In light of these contributions, it is not surprising why virtually every piece of legislation promoting stronger regulation of the for-profit education market has died after being referred to this committee. Examples of this include H.R. 6407-112, College Student Rebate Act of 2012, which was introduced by Rep. John Tierney (D), MA-6, on September 13, 2012. This bill was intended to compel for-profit colleges to allocate more funds toward student instruction and services. It would be accomplished by mandating that colleges could spend no less than 80 percent of its funds on student instruction and services.[44] H.R. 6407 also provided that any school that did not adhere by this new mandate would be forced to provide a rebate to students.[45] However, on the same day that this bill was introduced, it was referred to the House Committee on Education and the Workforce, where it died soon after.

Another similar instance surrounds H.R. 340-113, Protecting Financial Aid for Students and Taxpayers Act, which was introduced by Rep. Raul Grijalva (D), AZ-3, on January 22, 2013. Its intended objective was to restrict for-profit colleges from allocating revenue derived from federal education assistance programs toward advertising, marketing, and recruiting.[46] The bill was referred to the House Committee on Education and the Workforce, where it died soon after it entered committee.

These bills, which were intended to induce healthy regulations in the for-profit education market, are among a laundry list of legislative attempts that have been singlehandedly defeated by the House Committee on Education and the Workforce. No matter how great the efforts of student protection mavericks, such as Tom Harkin (D-IA), Kay Hagan (D-NC), Elizabeth Warren (D-MA), Richard Blumenthal (D-CT), and Dick Durbin (D-IL), regulations on this particular market are destined for defeat. This is expected to go unchanged so long as for-profit lobbying and campaign contributions effectively target key members who sit on the House Committee on Education and the Workforce. Nonetheless, academics and legislators should continue to propose helpful policy reforms with the hopes of eventually correcting this problem before it is too late.

ESSENTIAL TAKEAWAYS

As a direct result of its predatory behavior, for-profit firms have an incredible amount of money at stake. Reacting to the fierce criticism and public outcry stemming from the material presented in a series of reports filed through the Senate HELP Committee, for-profit higher-education companies launched an aggressive lobbying campaign with the assumed intention of blocking comprehensive reform that would have otherwise passed to correct the abuses that continue to take place.

It turns out, however, that the for-profit higher-education sector had to do relatively very little to achieve its objective. With the 535 members in both chambers of Congress, for-profit higher-education companies were able to block any significant measure of reform by heavily influencing only three members of the House with very crucial committee assignments. Consequently, reform proposals in the past, present, and future face a virtually impossible road to success. As a result, the status quo prevails, and millions of students continue to fall victim to the for-profit higher-education fraud.

9

ERADICATION

Considering the case that has just been argued against the for-profit industry, a quote by John D. Rockefeller seems relevant before addressing a solution: "I believe that every right implies a responsibility; every opportunity, an obligation; every possession, a duty."[1] What Rockefeller establishes is a social contract with the caveat that privileges demand accountability. Judging from the reports based on years of federal investigation into the industry proves that this concept does not exist in the for-profit higher-education market.

A possible explanation can be found in the core flaw of the for-profit higher-education model in that proprietary education companies use education as a means to generate higher profit margins, thus behaving with little to no regard for students. It has been made clear from the preceding discussion that for-profit colleges: first, use education as a means to generate profit; second, use deceptive practices in the pursuit of such profits; third, do so with significant financial assistance from the federal government; fourth, have negatively affected millions of students as a result; and, fifth, use those profits to block meaningful reform. It is also evident that modest regulations that have been placed on the industry by Congress not only fail to improve outcomes for students but also at times cause them to become even worse.

The for-profit crisis cannot be solved with a mere establishment of a "uniform methodology for calculating job placement rates" or "expanding the default reporting period."[2] Proposals of this degree, although politically viable, have proven to fail time and again. Amendments to the Higher Education Act that consider the default oversight timetable is a perfect example of this.[3] In 2008, Congress extended the two-year timetable to three years. What happened? GRC repayment plans diminish by 7 percent the year after, following a transfer of students into deferment or forbearance in order to keep the default rates artificially low. Can Congress honestly expect that a change from three to four years is going to have any better of an effect than the earlier change from two to three years? These recommendations, although carefully considered and politically savvy, are insufficient to curing the college market of the for-profit crisis. In order to ensure a return on an annual $32 billion federal investment, as well as to safeguard the security of millions of students each year, far bolder solutions are necessary.

Before we consider any of the politically viable methods for achieving a stronger response, the end objective of the proposal must be carefully deliberated. The industry displays an utter lack of consideration for the taxpayer investment, exhibits implacable contempt of the millions of people who are harmed each year by profit-oriented models, and conducts a continuous flow of efforts to circumvent government oversight. As a consequence, modest proposals have failed miserably.

Although the end objective is to transform the for-profit higher-education market as it exists today, there are several avenues, varying in degree of directness and severity, that could be embraced as the primary tool in changing the status quo. The first of these methods includes slightly more aggressive amendments to the Higher Education Act of 1965. These amendments would remove eligibility for "federal financial assistance programs under Title IV of the HEA" from the for-profit education companies that have been investigated and found guilty of predatory action.[4] The Higher Education Act defines *for-profit schools* as separate from nonprofit schools, dedicating two separate subsections to provide distinct definitions of each realm.

The first comes in §600.4(a): "An institution of higher education [is] a public or private nonprofit education institution."[5] The succeeding paragraphs of §600.5 highlight the distinction between nonprofit and for-profit education: "A proprietary [for-profit] institution of higher education is an educational institution that—(1) Is not a public or private nonprofit education institution."[6] The HEA, as it is written, recognizes the stark difference between traditional institutions of higher education and proprietary institutions of higher education.

Later, §600.7 details a specific set of conditions that, if not satisfied, revoke Title IV aid eligibility status from that respected institution in either category.[7] The first proposal is simple: Attach an amendment to §600.7 that unconditionally revokes Title IV aid eligibility from each of the firms that were indicted in the Senate HELP Committee reports. Section 600.7 already includes a list of exclusions that justify such a standard for revocation. For instance, §600.7(3)(ii) bars access of Title IV aid if the "institution, its owner, or its chief executive officer—has been judicially determined to have committed fraud involving title IV, HEA program funds."[8] Given the countless reports filed by both the Senate HELP Committee and the GAO, the for-profit higher-education firms that were investigated fail the spirit of the standard established by §600.7, regardless of the fact that they were found guilty through a series of legislative investigations and not the judicial system. From the conditions set out by the standard of §600.7, the legislative intent is to protect students and taxpayers from fraudulent activity in higher education.

Senator Dick Durbin described to ABC News that the conduct of the for-profit higher-education industry is "just plain fraud."[9] The fact that fraudulence is rampant throughout the for-profit higher-education market is irrefutable, given the thousands of pages of executive memos, internal management instruction manuals, and endless testimony in hearings on Capitol Hill. Given the *purpose* of §600.7, and after considering the specific provisions already laid out, there is a reasonable possibility that the investigated firms within the for-profit higher-education market would fail the intended standard if challenged judicially.

There have already been several settlements involving fraudulence suits against for-profit institutions, indicating that this supposition is warranted. For example, California's attorney general filed suit against Corinthian Colleges, Inc., in 2007, following an investigation revealing that the company significantly inflated its placement rates "by as much as 37 percent for every program examined." The suit ultimately resulted in the company paying $6.5 million to students and the state of California to settle the dispute.[10]

Eventually, Corinthian met its match when the Consumer Financial Protection Bureau filed a lawsuit[11] in response to complaints surrounding Corinthian's Genesis Lending Program. Typical of predatory lending in the for-profit higher-education sector, the Genesis Lending Program serviced institutional loans that carried interest rates of 15 percent with an origination fee of 6 percent.[12] By April 2015, as a result of several serious lawsuits, Corinthian Colleges Inc., announced that it would be shutting its doors for good and has since gone out of business.[13]

Alta Colleges, Inc., has faced several similar suits, the first occurring in 2009, when it paid the United States $7 million to settle allegations that it inflated its employment rates, advertising 90 percent job placement when the actual rate was 50 percent.[14] Another settlement followed in 2012, when Alta paid $4.5 million in damages to students and the state to settle a suit brought by Colorado's attorney general "alleging inflated placement statistics, deceptive advertising, misleading recruiting practices, and enrolling students in institutional loans without their knowledge."[15]

These settlements indicate that the companies involved had at least the potential to be judicially found in violation of §600.7(3)(ii) but avoided such rulings with settlements. Although this is a short-term victory to students who are awarded damages, large for-profit education companies continue to both receive Title IV funds and engage in the same questionable business practices because the settlements allow companies to ultimately circumvent being held to the §600.7 standard by the judiciary. Therefore, the only long-term solution that prevents future harm to students is to directly apply this standard to companies that have been found guilty of this practice because the judicial system has proven to be ineffective at holding for-profit companies accountable thus far.

However, this measure should not be limited exclusively to market giants, currently under the investigation of Congress. Every single college classified under §600.5 as a "proprietary institution" should be included under the exclusionary standard of the proposed amendment to §600.7. Accompanying this bold approach is the probability of pushback from critics, who may suggest that this is an anti–free market proposal that denies companies fair treatment, demanding that the smaller firms who have not been proven guilty of questionable practices are being snuffed out indiscriminately. These assertions, although understandable, fail to consider that each of these market "whales" originally started out as "minnows," much like many of the smaller companies today. For instance, Apollo Group, which enrolled approximately 470,800 students in 2010, began as an eight-student program in 1976.[16]

Now offering online degree programs in more than one hundred different fields, this goliath was first housed in a single room of Boilermakers' Union Hall in Phoenix, rented by founder John Sperling.[17] In other words, Apollo Group has transformed from a handful of amateurs into the nation's largest for-profit higher-education conglomerate. If only the largest for-profit firms are removed, what stops the current market minnows from simply replacing the old whales as the new ones? Nothing.

Although this latter step moves the status quo in the right direction, it does not completely fulfill the end objective of guaranteeing total protection from predatory action that derives from the for-profit market. Currently, federal taxpayer revenue funds 86 percent of the industry, approximately $32 billion in 2010 alone. By eliminating this source, Congress would effectively protect a majority of the people who are being harmed today but not all. The remaining 14 percent of the industry constitutes a market share of $5.2 billion, which is largely operated under high-interest institutional loans. By limiting measures taken against for-profit companies to taxpayer funds, there is still plenty of room for the for-profit industry to harm prospective students. Consequently, there is an additional step that is necessary to ensure the protection of students across the country from for-profit firms.

There is but one way to guarantee with absolute certainty the preservation of the public interest and the sanctity of higher education in the United States. The only sure answer that exists is to strip all companies that are classified under §600.5 as "proprietary institutions of higher education" of their legal capacity to operate. This would consequently eradicate them from the higher-education market altogether. However, there are several avenues to approach this from a legal standpoint, some having been declared unconstitutional by the Supreme Court. Therefore, it is worth examining the record of the judiciary on relevant cases before declaring our own course of action. Additionally, it is my purpose to prove not only that the court has upheld a constitutional standard in a few recent cases but also that the precedent established by the modern court reflects a far deeper understanding of the general relationship between the federal and state governments. To do so, our conversation begins in the spring of 1787.

Following the ratification of the Articles of Confederation six years earlier, the United States was on the brink of imploding. According to Alexander Hamilton, the federal government, which had initially been designed to function inadequately under the articles as a subordinate to the states, stood as a direct cause for this time of political and economic peril:

> The United States, as now composed, have no powers to exact obedience, or punish disobedience to their resolutions, either by pecuniary mulcts, by a suspension or divestiture of privileges, or by any other constitutional mode. *There is no express delegation of authority to them to sue force against delinquent members; and if such a right should be ascribed to the federal head*, as resulting from the nature of the social compact between the States, it must be by inference and construction in the face of that part of the second article by which it is declared "that each State shall retain every power, jurisdiction, and right, not expressly delegated to the United States in the Congress assembled." . . . *If we are unwilling to impair the force of this applauded provision, we shall be obliged to conclude, that the United States afford the extraordinary spectacle of a government destitute even of the shadow of constitutional power to enforce the execution of its own laws.* [18]

In order to address the inherent structural problems of the political processes that threatened to destroy the country from within, statesmen met in Philadelphia to draft what would eventually become the US Constitution. Following several months of debate over the summer of 1787, as well as two years of subsequent deliberation throughout the ratification process, Congress ultimately decided to fundamentally redefine the roll of the federal government forever.

The distinction between the openings of both documents is very telling of this point. Under Article I of the Articles of Confederation, "The style of this confederacy shall be, 'The United States of America.'" [19] The opening language of the United States Constitution employs drastically different language: "We the people of the United States, in Order to form a more perfect Union, establish Justice, insure domestic Tranquility, provide for the common defense, promote the general Welfare, and secure the Blessings of Liberty to ourselves and our Posterity, do ordain and establish this Constitution for the United States of

America."[20] Notice the profound change between the introductions of these two documents. While the former establishes a mere connection between a cluster of states, emphasizing a virtually unchecked degree of sovereignty as a result, the latter intentionally highlights the importance of "*We the people*" rather than *we the states*. Starting from the first three words of this new constitution, its framers establish that states would no longer be the focus of the new government. Operating under this newly established "*union of the people*," Madison wastes no time outlining an incredibly broad scope of federal objectives and powers, most notably being to "provide for the common defense" and to "promote the general Welfare." Under these two fundamental pillars of federal obligation, the framers outline a subsequent series of specifically enumerated powers to the federal government.

Although there was a large consensus between Federalists, including James Madison, Alexander Hamilton, and John Jay, that a strong federal government was necessary for the survival of the country, there was still a great deal of controversy concerning the *extent* of the powers given to this supreme body of government. The most basic component surrounding the extent of federal power is the understanding of the Tenth Amendment. It reads, "The powers not delegated to the United States by the Constitution, nor prohibited by it to the States, are reserved to the States respectively, or to the people."[21] As a consequence of the Tenth Amendment, any authority that is not specifically delegated to Congress is then passed on to state control by default. This places a direct and immediate check on the dominant scope of federal authority, as it limits at the surface which affairs the federal government can and cannot involve itself in. For example, because Congress is not expressly granted jurisdiction over educational affairs, states are given control over such matters.

Although there is almost universal agreement to this point, a broad and contentious debate over the federal government's role on these "state" affairs, using other clauses embedded within the Constitution, persists on nearly every other aspect of the discussion. Throughout the years of this ongoing debate, evaluations and interpretations have been many. Consequently, the place to begin our own analysis appropriately starts where the debate over this particular issue began: between James Madison and Alexander Hamilton.

Madison discusses this relationship in Federalist 39, examining the Constitution as both a federal and a national document. This distinction between a federal and national constitution can be put, in the simplest of terms, as a constitution reflecting a government that derives its power and exerts its authority in two fundamentally different principles. Under the *federal* mindset, the federal government derives its power from the individual states, therefore deferring greater power to the sovereign authority of the individual states.

Conversely, a *national* philosophy adopts the principle that the federal government receives its power not from the states but from the people of the collective body of states, therefore granting the federal government greater direct authority over affairs otherwise left primarily to the states. Although Madison ultimately concludes that the Constitution is "in strictness neither a national nor a federal constitution," he asserts that the "operation of the Government on the people in their individual capacities, in its ordinary and most essential proceedings, may on the whole designate it in this relation as a *national* government."[22] He goes on to explain that aside from the *operation* of its powers, there is the additional component of the "relation to the *extent* of its powers" as well.[23] Contrary to the *national* view that, when "all persons and things . . . are consolidated into one nation, this supremacy is completely vested in national Legislature," there is the *federal* view.[24] From this, the "local or municipal authorities form distinct and independent portions of the supremacy, no more subject within their respective spheres to the general authority, than the general authority is subject to them, within its own sphere."[25]

Recognizing that there are "independent portions of the supremacy" under the *federal* view, Madison concludes, "In this relation then, the proposed Government cannot be deemed a *national* one; since its jurisdiction extends to certain enumerated objects only, and leaves to the several States a residuary and inviolable sovereignty over all other objects."[26] As a result, there are conflicting applications to the *operation* and *extent* of national powers, the former being a *national* view and the latter adopting a *federal* view. In other words, Madison adopts the *national* notion that the federal government retains supremacy over the states on issues under their expressed jurisdiction. However, this is done with the *federal* caveat that matters not explicitly given to Congress are reserved to the states by default.

While Madison specifically refers to the Supremacy Clause found in Article IV, Section 2, this philosophy can be extended to other clauses embedded within the Constitution that had similar intended effects, such as the Commerce Clause or Spending Clause, both under Article I, Section 8.[27] This shift toward applying other clauses as justification for federal intervention has been popular because the Supremacy Clause has been limited to uphold specific protections against state law trumping federal law, like in the state taxing case of *McCulloch v. Maryland*.[28] The Commerce and Spending Clauses have been typically applied as direct validation for federal involvement and employed as a more solid defense for such intervention as a result.

In the December 5, 1791, "Report on Manufactures," Alexander Hamilton wholly contradicts the Madisonian proposition that there should be constrictive limits set on the scope and extent of federal involvement in state affairs. Referring to the "general welfare" pillar in the preamble of the Constitution, Hamilton reflects on the necessity of federal involvement in manufacturing and agricultural markets across the United States:

> The terms "general welfare" *were doubtlessly intended to signify more than was expressed or imported in those which preceded*; otherwise, numerous exigencies incident to the affairs of a nation would have been left without a provision. The phrase is as comprehensive as any that could have been used; because it was not fit that the constitutional authority of the Union to appropriate its revenues should have been restricted within narrower limits than the "general welfare;" and because this necessarily embraces a vast variety of particulars, which are susceptible neither of specification nor of definition. *It is, therefore, of necessity, left to the discretion of the National Legislature to pronounce upon the objects which concern the general welfare*, and for which, under that description, an appropriation of money is requisite and proper. And there seems to be no room for a doubt, that *whatever concerns the general interests* of learning, of agriculture, of manufactures, and of commerce, *are within the sphere of the national councils.*[29]

Hamilton simply asserts that the general welfare encompasses a broad range of topics that cannot and should not be limited by "specification nor of definition," proposing that the entire matter is left completely to the discretion of Congress. What Hamilton defines as being necessary and proper to promoting the general welfare of the country, Madison sees as a threat to the balance of good government. In Madison's words, Hamilton's proposals under the "Report on Manufactures" are guilty of

> subverting the fundamental and characteristic principle of the Government, as contrary to the true and fair, as well as the received construction, and as bidding defiance to the sense in which the Constitution is known to have been proposed, advocated and adopted. *If Congress can do whatever in their discretion can be done by money, and will promote the general welfare, the Government is no longer a limited one possessing enumerated powers, but an indefinite one subject to particular exceptions.*[30]

Madison reaffirms this in a letter to Andrew Stevenson on November 27, 1830, six years after the *Gibbons v. Ogden* case,[31] writing, "With respect to the words 'general welfare,' I have always regarded them as qualified by the detail of powers connected with them. To take them in a literal and unlimited sense would be a metamorphosis of the Constitution into a character when there is a host of proofs was not contemplated by its creators."[32]

Although Madison's rhetoric is compelling, the Hamiltonian mindset is aligned closer to the appropriate reading of the tools necessary to "provide for the common defense and promote the general welfare." In Federalist 22, Hamilton compares the trading inefficiencies of the Germanic states to those of America:

> The commerce of the German empire is in continual trammels from the multiplicity of the duties which the several princes and states exact upon the merchandises passing through their territories, by means of which the fine streams and navigable rivers with which Germany is so happily watered are *rendered almost useless.* Though the genius of the people of this country might never permit this description to be strictly applicable to us, yet we may reasonably expect, *from the gradual conflicts of State regulations, that the citizens of each would at length come to be considered and treated by the others in no better light than that of foreigners and aliens.*[33]

Hamilton proves the necessity for national coordination in the operation and exchange of interstate markets within the United States, highlighting the problems associated with trade among unconstrained states. This practical policy, based entirely on fulfilling objectives plainly stated in the Constitution, overwhelmingly trumps the Madisonian position, which is based primarily on theoretical reasoning that is derived from a fear of overcentralized government.

Both men believe that the federal government should "provide for the common defense and promote the general welfare." The difference between the two is that Hamilton promotes an interpretation that gives the federal government the capacity to fulfill these policy objectives, while Madison does not. Since this debate between Hamilton and Madison began, a majority of the discussion has focused on the extent to which Congress has the ability to constrain the application of the Tenth Amendment. Emerging as the two most viable options in their relevance to the topic, the Commerce Clause and Spending Clause have been examined by the court in their capacity to achieve this end.

In regard to the Commerce Clause, two relatively recent decisions by the Supreme Court explain why the Commerce Clause is not a viable option to pursue for our purposes. Ushering in what is referred to as the "anti-commandeering principle," *New York v. United States* and *Printz v. United States* are primarily responsible for placing limitations on the extent of the Commerce Clause in this regard.

Writing for the court in *New York v. United States*, Justice O'Connor expressed that "Congress may not simply . . . commandeer the legislative processes of the States by directly compelling them to enact and enforce a federal regulatory program."[34] Five years after *New York v. United States*, *Printz v. United States* helped to solidify this precedent of limiting the extent of the Commerce Clause. Writing for the court, Justice Scalia explained the court's extension of the precedent set by *New York v. United States*:

> We held in New York that *Congress cannot compel the States to enact or enforce a federal regulatory program. Today we hold that Congress cannot circumvent that prohibition by conscripting the State's officers directly*. The Federal Government may neither issue directives requiring the States to address particular problems, nor command the States' officers, or those of their political subdivisions, to administer or enforce a federal regulatory program. It matters not whether policymaking is involved, and no case by case weighing of the burdens or benefits is necessary; *such commands are fundamen-*

tally incompatible with our constitutional system of dual sovereign-
ty.[35]

Standing as the cornerstones of this relatively recent standard, *New York v. United States* and *Printz v. United States* apply a strict standard in limiting the capacity of the Commerce Clause. As a result, the Commerce Clause is not a viable avenue for upholding the constitutionality of my proposal, placing the fate of my proposal with the Spending Clause.

While the preceding cases diminish the strength of the Commerce Clause as justification for federal intervention in state affairs, they say nothing of restricting such action under the Spending Clause. As a result, Congress should implement a federal standard under the Spending Clause of the Constitution that would condition federal primary and secondary education funds on the states' compliance to place legal bans on the operation of for-profit higher-education companies in their respective borders. To do so, attention should be directed toward the Supreme Court precedent that has been set concerning issues surrounding the Spending Clause.

Our conversation begins in 1936 with the court's deliberation of *United States v. Butler*, a case upholding that the processing of taxes instituted under the 1933 Agricultural Adjustment Act were unconstitutional on the grounds of violating the Tenth Amendment.[36] Writing for the court, Justice Roberts declared, "The regulation of the farmer's activities under the statute, though in form subject to his own will, is, in fact, coercion through economic pressure; his right of choice is illusory," concluding that "Congress cannot invade state jurisdiction by purchasing the action of individuals any more than by compelling it."[37]

Although this seems to place a strict limit on the scope of the Spending Clause in its entirety, Butler went on to declare the Agricultural Adjustment Act unconstitutional on the specific grounds that the regulation of agriculture production was left to the states.[38] This narrow application, confined to agricultural production and not in a broader sense, captures the enduring principle that the court effectively embraced the Hamiltonian position and rejected Madison's. In doing so, the court found that the "power of Congress to authorize expenditure of public moneys for public purposes is not limited by the direct grants of legislative power found in the Constitutions," adding that the "spending power's confines are set in the clause which confers it, and not in those of Section 8 which bestow and define the legislative powers of the Congress."[39] The consequence of this decision recognizes the independent nature of Congress's taking and spending powers and ultimately lays the foundation for a series of cases to defend the natural autonomy of the Spending Clause.

The first of these subsequent cases came in 1937 with the ruling of *Steward Machine Company v. Davis*, a court ruling upholding that the tax under the Social Security Act was a constitutional exercise of congressional power.[40] Delivering the opinion of the court, Justice Cardozo explained, "There must be a showing in the first place that separated from the credit the revenue provisions are incapable of standing by themselves. There must be a showing in the second place that the tax and the credit in combination are weapons of coercion, destroying or impairing the autonomy of the states" in order for the federal action to be protected against under the Tenth Amendment.[41] In this maneuver by the court, the scope of the Spending Clause was bolstered to the point of having the capacity of inducing states to adopt federal standards.

Continuing the direction of *Steward Machine Company v. Davis*, the most relevant case of Spending Clause milestones is *South Dakota v. Dole*. Although this case was centered on the national drinking age and not issues surrounding for-profit higher education, *South Dakota v. Dole* still supports the structural pillars of my proposal to induce states into banning for-profit higher education. In 1984, Congress passed the National Minimum Drinking Age Act, which withheld 5 percent of federal highway funding from states that did not maintain a minimum legal drinking age of 21. South Dakota, which allowed nineteen-year-olds to purchase beer containing up to 3.2 percent alcohol, challenged the law, naming Secretary of Transportation Elizabeth Dole as the respondent.[42] Writing for the court, Justice Rehnquist first established that the Twenty-first Amendment "confirms the States' broad power to impose restrictions on the sale and distribution of alcoholic beverages."[43] Although Rehnquist affirmed that issues related to the drinking age are yielded to state control, he argued that it "does not confer on them any power to permit sales that Congress seeks to prohibit it," nor does it "prevent Congress from affirmatively enacting a national minimum drinking age more restrictive than that provided by the various state laws; and it would follow a fortiori that the indirect inducement involved here is compatible with the Twenty-first Amendment."[44] In other words, the drinking age is a matter left to be handled by the state, but the federal government may induce the state to adopt a federal drinking age standard. However, the most significant part of this opinion is that Rehnquist laid out a set of criteria that established four caveats to the constitutionality of Spending Clause application:

> The *first* of these limitations is derived from the language of the Constitution itself: the exercise of the spending power must be in pursuit of "the general welfare." In considering whether a particular expenditure is intended to serve general public purposes, courts should defer substantially to the judgment of Congress. *Second*, we have required that if Congress desires to condition the States' receipt of federal funds, it "must do so unambiguously . . . , enabling the States to exercise their choice knowingly, cognizant of the consequences of their participation." *Third*, our cases have suggested (without significant elaboration) that conditions on federal grants might be illegitimate if they are unrelated "to the federal interest in particular national projects or programs." *Finally*, we have noted that other constitutional provisions may provide an independent bar to the conditional grant of federal funds.[45]

In essence, as long as Congress is acting on behalf of the general welfare of the country and it is clear that funds are conditioned, that the funds are related to the mandate, and that the funds do not extend so large as to become coercive, the Spending Clause allows Congress to condition funds in order to induce states to adopt a federal standard.

The key distinction between the Commerce Clause and Spending Clause is that the Commerce Clause does not give states a choice in the matter; they are simply mandated to act in a way that Congress instructs them to. The Spending Clause is not treated with the same scrutiny as the Commerce Clause because the state may refuse to accept the federal funds if it does not wish to comply with the federal mandate. Prominent constitutional law scholar, Erwin Chemerinsky best explains this distinction: "If Congress is clear the receipt of funds entails a waiver of sovereign immunity, then by accepting the money, a state has, by definition, consented to suit."[46] He expands on this notion in describing a case from the Eighth Circuit Court of Appeals, which "considered whether Arkansas had waived its sovereign immunity by receiving funds under section 504 of the Rehabilitation Act of 1973."[47] The court recognized the principle that states do, in fact, enter into a waiver of sovereign immunity after acceptance of federal funds:

> The Arkansas Department of Education can avoid the requirements of Section 504 simply by declining federal funds. The sacrifice of all federal education funds, approximately $250 million or 12 percent of the annual state education budget . . . , would be politically painful, but we cannot say that it compels Arkansas's choice. . . . The choice is up to the State: either give up federal aid to education, or agree that the Department of Education can be sued under Section 504. We think the Spending Clause allows Congress to present States with this sort of choice.[48]

The Eighth Circuit Court of Appeals, like the Supreme Court in *South Dakota v. Dole*, recognized the difference between inducement and coercion. If a state decides that it would rather sacrifice federal funds to uphold its sovereign immunity to have total control on that given matter, then that is the state's choice. As the opinion in *Steward Machine Company v. Davis* recognized, "To hold that motive or temptation is equivalent to coercion is to plunge the law into endless difficulties. The outcome of such a doctrine is the acceptance of a philosophical determinism by which choice becomes impossible."[49]

Consequently, the Spending Clause has been distinguished from the Commerce Clause as having more expansive authority in respect to the extent of power it controls. Unfortunately, a recent decision delivered by the Supreme Court presents the potential for such "endless difficulties" in muddying this seemingly simple standard that has been applied since 1936. In the 2012 case *National Federation of Independent Business v. Sebelius*, Chief Justice Roberts expressed in the majority opinion, "Congress may use its spending power to create incentives for States to act in accordance with federal policies. But when 'pressure turns to compulsion,' the legislation runs contrary to our system of federalism."[50] Justice Ginsburg's opinion summarized the subsequent overarching claims made by Roberts in his opinion:

> His conclusion rests on three premises, each of them essential to his theory. First, the Medicaid expansion is, in The Chief Justice's view,

a new grant program, not an addition to the Medicaid program existing before the ACA's enactment. Congress, The Chief Justice main-
tains, has threatened States with the loss of funds from an old program in an effort to get them to adopt a new one. Second, the
expansion was unforeseeable by the States when they first signed on
to Medicaid. Third, the threatened loss of funding is so large that the
States have no real choice but to participate in the Medicaid expansion.[51]

The substance of the first two premises are more exclusively concerned
with the Medicaid expansion provisions of the Affordable Care Act.
However, the last of the three premises is incredibly important to our
discussion, as it "for the first time ever—finds an exercise of Congress'
spending power unconstitutionally coercive."[52]

Establishing that "Spending Clause programs do not pose this dan-
ger when a State has a legitimate choice whether to accept the federal
conditions in exchange for federal funds," Chief Justice Roberts distinguished that "in the typical case we look to the States to defend their
prerogatives by adopting 'the simple expedient of not yielding' to federal blandishments when they do not want to embrace the federal policies
as their own."[53] Recognizing that the "Medicaid expansion is far from
the typical case," Chief Justice Roberts ultimately addressed his third
premise by explaining the financial intricacies of the Medicaid expansion. With the implementation of the Medicaid expansion, "Congress
will pay 90 percent of the costs for newly eligible persons," which today
"accounts for over 20 percent the average States total budget."[54] This
means that approximately 19 percent of each state's budget will be
stripped under §1396c of the Affordable Care Act upon failing to comply with the Medicaid expansion plan. Comparing this to the threatened
loss of "less than half of one percent of South Dakota's budget in *South
Dakota v. Dole*, Chief Justice Roberts concluded that "this threatened
loss of a State's overall budget, in contrast, is economic dragooning that
leaves the States with no real option but to acquiesce in the Medicaid
expansion."[55]

Although Chief Justice Roberts asserted that the encouragement
under Congress's Spending Clause in this case goes "beyond" the line, a
line for which its criteria he failed to explicitly outline, Justice Ginsburg
and Justice Scalia profoundly disagreed that any such line can be found
in the court's precedent. Justice Ginsburg insisted, "Congress must of

course have authority to impose limitations on the States' use of the federal dollars. This Court, time and again, has respected Congress' prescription of spending conditions, and has required States to abide by them."[56]

Contradicting Chief Justice Roberts, Justice Ginsburg went on to include that "there are federalism-based limits on the use of Congress' conditional spending power," which are expressed in *South Dakota v. Dole*, concluding that "prior to today's decision, the Court has never ruled that the terms of any grant crossed the indistinct line between temptation and coercion."[57]

Justice Scalia reinforced Justice Ginsburg's attention to *Dole* by quoting that "objectives not thought to be within Article I's enumerated legislative fields, may nevertheless be attained through the use of the spending power and the conditional grant of federal funds."[58] From this, Justice Scalia joined Ginsburg in the sentiment that "when Congress makes grants to the States, it customarily attaches conditions, and this Court has long held that the Constitution generally permits Congress to do this."[59]

In addition to Justice Ginsburg and Justice Scalia refuting Chief Justice Roberts's perception of court precedent, it is also worth noting the foundational claim to Roberts's argument that the "Constitution simply does not give Congress the authority to require the States to regulate"[60] is pulled from *New York v. United States*. However, as we have already discovered,[61] *New York v. United States* concerns the Commerce Clause, not the Spending Clause. Nevertheless, Chief Justice Roberts's remarks still stand as the majority opinion and must be duly treated as court precedent as a result.

Although *Sebelius* stands as a limit on the exercise of Congress's spending power, the financial substance of my proposal is more consistent, in respect to being a burden on state budgets, with *Dole* than it is with *Sebelius*. While states spend roughly the same amount of money on Medicaid as they do education, the federal proportion to each of these expenditures is vastly different. Compared to the 90 percent of federal financial coverage to Medicaid following the expansion program, only an average of 13 percent of education expenditures in state budgets are derived from federal aid.[62] This means that, while states would sacrifice approximately 19 percent of their entire budget upon failure to comply with the Medicaid expansion program, states would only lose a maximum of 3 percent of their total budgets by failing to adopt the federal standard of outlawing the practice of proprietary higher-education institutions.

Considering both the specific arguments made by the court in the Spending Clause cases, as well as the substance of my proposals in relation to these arguments, there is but one conclusion that can be drawn. Provisions to withhold primary and secondary education funds to any state that does not comply with the federal standard to ban the practice of institutions classified under §600.5 of the Higher Education Act as a "proprietary institution of higher education" are entirely constitutional.

ESSENTIAL TAKEAWAYS

In response to predatory behavior found in several investigations filed by the Senate Committee on Health, Education, Labor, and Pensions as well as the Government Accountability Office, Congress has made modest attempts to curb the behavior of for-profit colleges. However, rather than helping students, many of these measures have either failed to make the situation better or, at times, have actually had an even worse effect on students.

Due to the degree of fraud and track record of the industry, I not only propose to strip for-profit higher education of federal funding, but I also ultimately suggest that Congress should induce states to adopt a federal standard that outlaws the practice of for-profit higher education in America. Under the precedent of *South Dakota v. Dole* and other cases like it, this can be done by conditioning federal K–12 education funds to states that do not comply under the Spending Clause. Given the repercussions of losing these federal funds, states would be inclined to adopt the federal standard, thus eradicating for-profit higher education in the United States as it exists today.

10

DIPLOMAS FOR JOBS, NOT PINK SLIPS

Although the federal government is constitutionally justified to condition money given to states for primary and secondary education, the question over the impact of such conditioning remains. According to the National Center for Education Statistics, funds derived from the federal government account for 13 percent of primary and secondary education expenditures nationwide.[1] This average has been calculated based on the range of funding accepted by each of the fifty states. For example, while federal funding accounted for the highest portion of any state education budget in South Dakota, at 16.4 percent, New Jersey accounted for the lowest percentage of its funds from the federal government, at 4.1 percent.[2] Although figures ranging from 4.1 percent to 16.4 percent appear to be small enough to have little effect if stripped from state education budgets, think again.

Amid recent extensive state budget cuts across the country, school districts have seen a significant drop in state funding, which accounts for approximately 43 percent of primary and secondary education funding nationwide.[3] As less money is flowing into the coffers via state funds, the proportion of federal funding to state funding increases significantly, creating a higher reliance on the sustainment of federal funds as a result.

Even without the withdrawal of federal education funds, states are facing significant budget problems in light of widespread state education budget cuts. As these budget cuts are being put into effect, school districts in poor urban and rural areas are facing particularly difficult circumstances. This is the case due to the way we finance American education today. Ultimately, primary and secondary education funds flow from three sources: local taxes, state funds, and federal aid. As the NCES report stated, "Property taxes support most of the funding that local government provides for education. Local governments collect taxes from residential and commercial properties as a direct revenue source for the local school district."[4] This creates a scenario where wealthier communities with higher property value have an advantage in tax collection compared to poor urban and rural localities with less of a property tax base. Consequently, poor communities are more reliant on state and federal aid than districts with a significant local property tax base. As the report concluded, "This can often mean that children who live in low-income communities with the highest needs go to schools with the least resources, the least qualified teachers, and substandard school facilities."[5]

Due to recent state budget cuts, this phenomenon is steadily becoming more regular. During a recent Pennsylvania State budget cycle, William Hite, superintendent of the Philadelphia School District, was quoted as saying that the board of education is "out of time and out of options" and was forced to solve the district's budget gap by closing thirty-seven schools the following year.[6] When all was said and done, "44 schools [were] closed or relocated and nearly two dozen more [underwent] grade changes," affecting more than 17,000 children in the Philadelphia area alone.[7]

While poor urban and rural districts are feeling the financial pains of recent state budget cuts more than their affluent suburban counterparts, no district has had immunity to these cutbacks. Recent state budget cuts in Wisconsin have "reduced state aid designed to equalize funding across school districts by $740 million over the current two-year budget cycle, a cut of 8 percent. The budget also reduces K–12 funds for services for at-risk children, school nursing, and alternative education."[8]

Mississippi faced the same hard decisions when its state department of education was forced to lay off 2,060 school employees "(704 teachers, 792 teacher assistants, 163 administrators, counselors, and librarians, and 401 bus drivers, custodians, and clerical personnel)" in order to balance school budgets.[9] Louisiana has dealt with this problem not by cutting the number of teachers or librarians but by scaling back

funding to the minimum levels, as determined by legal requirements of
the state's education finance formula, to programs that "ensure adequate support for at-risk and special needs students."[10]

With school budgets being slashed by state deficits, we gain a
glimpse of the consequences that could come in the aftermath of the
federal government withdrawing its average 13 percent in aid to state
school budgets. Although it is not likely that entire schools would be
closed down in every school district, it is likely that a withdrawal in
federal aid would have the capability of reaching virtually every school
district in every corner of the country in one way or another.

These cuts would spur further layoffs to teachers, driving class sizes
from the teens and twenties to levels possibly well into the thirties and
beyond. While enrichment programs for advanced students would be
obliterated, dwindling services like teaching assistants and vocational
therapists would harm thousands of at-risk or special needs children. As
electives ranging from band to home and careers would be all but
erased, extracurricular activities ranging from clubs to athletic programs
would also be likely victims of the new wave of cuts.

The predictable backlash from public outcry and retaliation from
powerful teachers' unions, like the National Education Association
(NEA) or American Federation of Teachers (AFT), would be insurmountable for state lawmakers if these consequences were to become a
reality for the sake of protecting the practice of for-profit higher education under claims of sovereign immunity.

Given the financial problems that state school budgets already face
across the country, in addition to the hypothetical nightmare that awaits
if federal funding is to be cut altogether, there is a high probability that
states would be swayed to waive their sovereign immunity on issues
surrounding the for-profit higher-education market in order to remain
eligible for federal primary and secondary education funding.

Understanding that the conditions on federal primary and secondary
education funds will likely be successful in the inducement of states to
place legal bans on the operation of institutions that are classified under
§600.5 of the Higher Education Act, there will be approximately $32
billion of federal revenue no longer designated to fund a for-profit
industry that does not exist. The next step of this process is to determine an objective for any new programs that are to be established and

to deploy this $32 billion of untied capital in a way that most efficiently reaches that objective.

While there will likely be recommendations for this money to be allocated toward offsetting the budget deficit, funding other programs, and so on, such proposals would be ill-considered. Given the incredible benefit that these programs can deliver to the American economy through funding efficient and inexpensive federally subsidized higher-education programs, I believe that these funds should and will ultimately remain directed at the federal higher-education initiative. Such funds would ultimately be committed to offering programs for prospective students who could benefit from vocational training in technical job fields that are in increasingly high demand.

Currently, prospective students are attracted to for-profit colleges with ads that promise job training and career services support that will quickly lead to employment as a skilled professional in a technical field that holds high market demand and a low supply of labor. This leads me to believe that the majority of prospective students who are likely to enroll in these new programs will come directly from the 12 percent of the college student market currently serviced by the for-profit sector.

To fill this demand, why not simply fund a program that fulfills the broken promises of the for-profit industry? The prospective students of this category seek quick employment after fulfilling a period of straight-forward job training, while many emerging industries, facing shortages in specialized labor, seek to fill these positions as quickly as possible. This simple and efficient objective stands as the best possible way to return both the student investment and respond to job market demand.

With the objective clearly defined as supporting the mutual interests of college students seeking employment as well as growing job markets demanding a larger skilled labor force, the focus now shifts to the task of creating a system that efficiently facilitates this vision. Once the for-profit industry has been eliminated, there will be three classifications of remaining college institutions that could serve as possible sites to absorb a government program with the intended outcomes previously outlined. These include four-year private nonprofit universities, four-year public state schools, and two-year public community colleges.

Based on an array of factors ranging from cost to curriculum similarities, community colleges stand out as the most appropriate place to adopt and develop these programs. Consequently, programs that are funded by revenue previously designated to the for-profit industry will consist of curriculum, with an emphasis on job market orientation, and be housed at community colleges across the country.

Recognizing both a necessity for programs with job market demand as well as the advantages that community colleges offer over others, President Obama has proposed "The American Graduation Initiative," which is virtually identical to my own vision of what these programs can and should do. In his opening remarks on this proposal, President Obama expressed the very sentiments that I have reiterated throughout this section: "Now is the time to build a firmer, stronger foundation for growth that will not only withstand future economic storms, but one that helps us thrive and compete in a global economy. It's time to reform our community colleges so that they provide Americans of all ages a chance to learn the skills and knowledge necessary to compete for the jobs of the future."[11]

Following this straightforward explanation for why such an initiative is necessary, President Obama went on to include an array of reasons community colleges are the preferred location to house these programs:

> Community colleges are the largest part of our higher education system, enrolling more than 6 million students, and growing rapidly. They feature affordable tuition, open admission policies, flexible course schedules, and convenient locations, and they are particularly important for students who are older, working, need remedial classes, or can only take classes part-time. They are also capable of working with businesses, industry and government to create tailored training programs to meet economic needs such as nursing, health information technology, advanced manufacturing, and green jobs, and of providing customized training at the worksite.[12]

The president concluded the rollout of his plan by discussing how business and industry are instrumental to "training the workforce of the future and meeting the on-going demands of the marketplace," highlighting that "many community colleges are already working with businesses to develop programs and classes ranging from degrees to certified training courses for retraining and on-going training for enhancing skills."[13] In other words, this philosophy not only has the potential to efficiently utilize the resources of community colleges, but it also has already proven so to a degree.

In addition to community colleges being tailored to have the capacity of working closely with businesses, there is also the issue of identifying which industries college programs should be partnering with. When establishing and developing curriculum for these objectives, how will these community colleges know which industries to target and the subsequent businesses to collaborate with as a result? The answer lies in an already-established network of sophisticated data collection that is facilitated by the US Bureau of Labor Statistics (BLS), a subsidiary of the US Department of Labor.

The BLS currently collects and organizes employment data from across the entire country, having the capacity to map trends of job growth and decline for particular industries and regions throughout the nation. Table 6 under the "Economic News Release" of the BLS, for example, charts out the thirty occupations with the largest projected employment growth between 2010 and 2020.[14] Similarly, Table 8, under the same section, lists the top thirty occupations with the largest projected employment decline over the same period.[15]

Additionally, the BLS has the capacity to also map out occupational employment by specific regions as well. For instance, by simply typing "Rochester, NY" into the database, information on every field of occupation in the surrounding Rochester area is clearly listed with a set of relevant statistics. This is incredibly useful material for community colleges to have when constructing programs tailored to satisfy employment trends in a given region because specific industries can be closely monitored by the click of a button once the BLS has collected and organized the material.

Continuing the focus on Rochester, NY, let us assume that curriculum development personnel at Monroe Community College (MCC), a two-year public school based out of Rochester, wanted to know if it would be a good investment to offer certification programs in computer systems analytics. Upon reviewing BLS data compiled from the Rochester area, occupation code "15-1121: Computer Systems Analysts" reveals that there are 2,040 people employed in this profession in the Rochester area, which is an 8.6 percent increase from the previous year.[16] It also highlights a median hourly wage of $32.34, or an annual mean salary of $68,850, which has risen by 2.5 percent from the previous year.[17] Considering the recent and projected growth, as well as the current mean salary for those employed in this field in the Rochester area, MCC would most likely allocate resources to offer professional certification programs in this area of study.

To this point, we have identified an employment-based objective for the programs proposed to replace the higher-education market share of the eliminated for-profit industry. Operating through the uniquely flexible components of community colleges, which are significantly more desirable than the more rigid structure of four-year state and private institutions, the location where these programs are to be offered has also been determined. Additionally, we have also identified a reliable source of data at the BLS, which will guide community colleges to make the correct investments in curriculum based on job market demand specifically tailored to their immediate regions.

The final two components to this government initiative is that of how these programs will be funded, as well as the structure of their administration to students. It is here that President Obama's proposal and my own take sharply different directions moving forward. In terms of funding, President Obama is calling for an "additional 5 million community college degrees and certificates by 2020," which will collectively cost $12 billion over the course of the next decade.[18] An example of financial initiatives being put forward is the expansion of Pell grants and college tax credits under the Community College to Career Fund Act.[19] To pay for this, the president is proposing a series of additional federal funds via "waste [spending] cuts from the student loan program, increases in Pell Grant scholarships, and reductions in the deficit."[20] While we should encourage cuts in waste spending from the student loan program, there are other sources of possible revenue that are being overlooked.

Rather than adopting the president's financial proposal that calls for a $12 billion investment over the course of a decade, there is a far more secure path to be considered. What the president's proposal fails to consider is the $32 billion of federal capital that would become available as a result of the liquidation of the for-profit higher-education industry. With this massive source of revenue, the federal government would be able to allocate $32 billion annually to programs at community colleges.

In addition to the differences between the size and method of financing the president's American Graduation Initiative, I have a somewhat different approach on how these programs should be run. The president has promoted and continues to promote strong support for a community college system that extensively incorporates online courses into the curriculum map:

> Online educational software has the potential to help students learn more in less time than they would with traditional classroom instruction alone. Interactive software can tailor instruction to individual students like human tutors do, while simulations and multimedia software offer experiential learning. Online instruction can also be a powerful tool for extending learning opportunities to rural areas or working adults who need to fit their coursework around families and jobs. New open online courses will create new routes for students to gain knowledge, skills and credentials.[21]

Supporting President Obama are reports filed by notable sources, such as the Bill and Melinda Gates Foundation, which have tried to highlight the advantages of online education as being cheaper, offering more access, and even holding interactive superiority relative to traditional face-to-face courses. A report from the "Complete College Georgia Plan," for example, called for institutions to "increase the array of online programs . . . to enable all students . . . to effectively pursue college completion."[22] However, Robert Jenkins of the *Chronicle of Higher Education* explained the fundamental flaw in this reasoning:

> At first glance, the idea seems to make a lot of sense: Surely if we make it easier for students to get the credits they need by offering as many classes as possible online, more will finish. And no doubt that approach is cost-effective, at least in the short run. We can increase access without having to spend money upfront for infrastructure— money that, incidentally, we don't have. We can also reach potential student populations whose only access to college courses comes via the Internet. *Unfortunately, we seem to have forgotten that access and completion are not the same thing.*[23]

Additionally, online supporters point to a 2009 report filed by the US Department of Education that concerns the effectiveness of online education. The report intended to illustrate that online courses are cheaper, more convenient, and have greater success with student outcomes. Analyzing ninety-nine individual studies of online learning conducted since 1996, the report concluded that "on average, students in online learning conditions performed better than those receiving face-to-face instruction."[24]

Although the Department of Education is generally a reliable source for information, several subsequent reports investigating the specific details of this narrative have stripped away nearly all credibility from the 2009 pro-online report. In an investigation titled "Effectiveness of Fully Online Courses for College Students: Response to a Department of Education Meta-Analysis," Shanna Smith Jaggers and Thomas Bailey of the Community College Research Center at Columbia University exposed fundamental flaws to the online-advocacy report. The first component of the investigation revealed that "only 28 of the 99 studies examined in the Education Department report focused on courses that were fully online. Furthermore, only seven looked at semester-long courses, as opposed to short-term online programs on narrow topics, 'such as how to use an Internet search engine.'"[25] Because only a fraction of the studies concerned courses that were both entirely online and a full semester long, the completion rates of the findings were artificially inflated relative to reality.

Moreover, Jenkins went on to additionally explain that these studies were "conducted at midsize or large universities, five of which were rated as 'selective' or 'highly selective' by U.S. News & World Report."[26] This point revealed that not only did the report manipulate its findings based on the type of the online course, but it also misrepresented the effectiveness of online courses at the average community college by testing it on students who are not generally attracted to community colleges, being that community colleges house many "at-risk students" and are not generally "highly selective."[27]

Jenkins made the final point that "in six of the seven studies, withdrawal rates were not even mentioned, meaning that the research gauged only how well students performed after completing the course. The studies didn't tell us anything about those students who didn't complete the course."[28] In essence, the major reports supporting the merits of online education not only manipulated data with variables that are inconsistent with community colleges, but they also deliberately focused on access and the narrow proportion of students who are able to complete the course, while simultaneously neglecting the broad number of students who withdrew before completion.

Although the investigated report failed to accurately portray the effects of online education, additional studies by researchers at Columbia's Community College Research Center have since revealed statistics concerning online college completion. Reported by the *Chronicle of Higher Education* in July 2012, the most recent study has "followed the enrollment history of 51,000 community-college students in the state of Washington between 2004 and 2009 [and] found an eight percentage-point gap in completion rates between traditional and online courses."[29] These findings confirm an earlier study filed in 2010 that examined community college students in Virginia, which found that "regardless of their initial level of preparation . . . students were more likely to fail or withdraw from online courses than from face-to-face courses."[30]

Despite the legitimate concerns raised by Jenkins and others, none of these reports refute the point that it is cheaper to administer online programs relative to traditional face-to-face courses. This is the case because the operational costs, ranging in everything from the physical space of the classroom, equipment, instructor office hours, and the like, are far more costly than setting up an online course where the student does almost all of the work independently and simply submits it online for grading. Although operational costs have proven to be lower for online programs, a recent study at the University of Rochester's Warner School of Education further questions the net benefit of an online program to students.

Supporting earlier studies that prove widespread gaps in graduation rates between brick-and-mortar and online courses, the study empirically revealed how physical detachment, inherent to online education, has negative consequences for students.[31] Guiffrida, Lynch, Wall, and Abel revealed that in addition to "competence" and "autonomy," a "relatedness to faculty" stands as one of the most significant factors in positive academic outcomes.[32] This evaluation confirms earlier observations made from the for-profit industry in that the average for-profit withdrawal rate of students enrolled in campus-based courses amounted to 44 percent, while 69.5 percent of students enrolled in online courses failed to complete their programs.[33] This does not mean that the online programs of today are not subject to modification in the future. However, given the fundamental difference between the "distance learning" of online education and the "relatedness to faculty" through personal and physical interaction, I am skeptical that modifications to online programs will be capable of overcoming these challenges.

Despite the current obsession with adopting online curriculum models as the future of education, the only proven benefit of such programs is that online courses are cheaper to operate than traditional face-to-face courses on campuses. Although online programs create greater access to students, we should be careful not to interchange *access* for *success*, as demonstrated by the several reports that focus on student outcomes compared between campus-based and online programs. Therefore, I would strongly suggest avoiding a model that adopts online learning as the cornerstone of any program's curriculum map.

With an objective, funding, and format in place, this chapter provides an image of what higher education in America could be for millions of students each year. As a nation, we have the capacity to make the reforms necessary to ensure the well-being of students and the societal interests of taxpayers. All we must do now is to act on what we know to be right.

ESSENTIAL TAKEAWAYS AND FINAL THOUGHTS

Based on the evidence offered by several reports from the Senate Committee on Health, Education, Labor, and Pensions, the for-profit higher-education industry has been found guilty of practices that are so deeply embedded, broadly accepted, and harmful to students that I believe it is beyond saving. Consequently, I have proposed to remove this destructive component from the higher-education market, with the hopes of redirecting federal funds that are currently allocated to a failed system into programs that are both affordable to the student and responsive to job market demand.

Under these programs, designed to promote the mutual interests of both students and employers, the federal investment in higher education will once again see a return on its investment in the form of diplomas for jobs and not pink slips. Rather, the system that I have outlined will work to benefit both the individual and society, all in the same effort toward reforming higher education in a way that guides people into secure and well-paying jobs through a simple and affordable college process.

Given the immense obstacles that for-profit higher education pose in the midst of seeking such reforms, there is no other option than to eliminate them altogether. By doing so, we will make a promise to students and taxpayers alike that investments on both of their behalves will be made not to fill the deep pockets of higher-education corporations. Rather, we will finally make good on the promise that, by investing in higher education, both the individual as well as the greater good of society will benefit.

In the case that the proposals outlined in the book are not adopted, for whatever reason, there is something that each and every one of us can do to work toward progress on this issue. Equipped with the knowledge that has been outlined in the preceding chapters, each of us can work to educate the world around us of the injustice and corruption that exists in for-profit higher education. Tell your family members about the problems that exist; discourage a neighbor from starting an online degree at a for-profit college; write a column for a local newspaper to inform others of the abuses that exist. Do something, anything, to inform the world around you that for-profit higher education has defrauded taxpayers and ruined millions of lives that have fallen victim to their tactics. By doing so, America will be one step closer to restoring an honest higher-education system that promotes the rebuilding of the middle class, making the American dream once again a reality.

NOTES

FOREWORD

1. Frederick Rudolph, *The American College and University: A History* (Athens, Georgia: University of Georgia Press, 1962), 48–49.

INTRODUCTION

1. Michelle Jamrisko and Ilan Kolet, "Cost of College Degree in U.S. Soars 12 Fold: Chart of the Day," *BloombergBusiness*, August 15, 2012, accessed August 20, 2013, http://www.bloomberg.com/news/2012-08-15/cost-of-college-degree-in-u-s-soars-12-fold-chart-of-the-day.html.

2. Jeffrey Sparshott, "Congratulations, Class of 2015. You're the Most Indebted Ever (For Now)," *Wall Street Journal*, May 8, 2015, accessed June 12, 2015, http://blogs.wsj.com/economics/2015/05/08/congratulations-class-of-2015-youre-the-most-indebted-ever-for-now.

3. Adam Levin, "Is College Tuition the Next Bubble?" *ABC News*, March 24, 2012, accessed August 20, 2013, http://abcnews.go.com/Business/bubble-time-cap-college-tuition/story?id=15987539.

I. THE FOR-PROFIT FRAMEWORK

1. Kevin Kinser, *From Main Street to Wall Street: The Transformation of For-Profit Higher Education* (San Francisco: Jossey-Bass, 2006), 13.

2. Ibid.

3. J. S. Brubacher and W. Rudy, *Higher Education in Transition: A History of American Colleges and Universities*, 4th ed. (New Brunswick, NJ: Transaction, 2008), 30.

4. David F. Labaree, "The Power of the Parochial in Shaping the American System of Higher Education," *Stanford University School of Education, Educational Research: The Importance and Effects of Institutional Spaces, Springer Science and Business Media Dordrecht* (2013), 31.

5. Brubacher and Rudy, *Higher Education in Transition*, 19.

6. Labaree, "Power of the Parochial," 31.

7. Ibid.

8. Ibid., 32.

9. Brubacher and Rudy, *Higher Education in Transition*, 13.

10. Ibid.

11. "Industrial Revolution," *History Channel*, 2013, accessed November 22, 2013, http://www.history.com/topics/industrial-revolution.

12. Kinser, *Main Street to Wall Street*, 17.

13. Ibid.

14. C. G. Reigner, *Beginnings of the Business School* (Baltimore, MD: H. M. Rowe, 1959).

15. Kinser, *Main Street to Wall Street*, 18.

16. C. A. Herrick, *Meaning and Practice of Commercial Education* (New York: Macmillan, 1904).

17. Reigner, *Beginnings of the Business School*.

18. Kinser, *Main Street to Wall Street*, 18.

19. Ibid., 19.

20. Grant Venn, *Man, Education and Work: Postsecondary Vocational and Technical Education* (Washington, DC: American Council on Education, 1964).

21. Kinser, *Main Street to Wall Street*, 20.

22. J. B. Lee and J. P. Merisotis, *Proprietary Schools: Programs, Policies, and Prospects*, ASHE-ERIC Higher Education Report no. 5 (Washington, DC: George Washington University, School of Education and Human Development, 1990).

23. Kinser, *Main Street to Wall Street*, 21.

24. Ibid.

25. Ibid.

26. Ibid., 22.

27. Ibid.

28. Andreas Ortmann, *Capital Romance: Why Wall Street Fell in Love with Higher Education* (Published online: Education Economics, 2001).

29. Kinser, *Main Street to Wall Street*, 25.

30. J. W. Miller and W. J. Hamilton, *The Independent Business School in American Education* (New York: McGraw-Hill, 1964).

31. Kinser, *Main Street to Wall Street*, 26.

32. J. P. Merisotis and J. M. Shedd, *Classification Systems for Two-Year Colleges* (San Francisco: Jossey-Bass, 2003).

33. Kinser, *Main Street to Wall Street*, 28.

34. Ibid.

35. Ibid.

36. Ibid., 29.

37. Ibid.

38. United States Senate Health, Education, Labor, and Pensions Committee (US Senate HELP Committee), *For Profit Higher Education: The Failure to Safeguard the Federal Investment and Ensure Student Success*, Majority Committee Staff Report and Accompanying Minority Committee Staff Views, July 30, 2012, 1.

39. Ibid., 20.

40. Suzanne Mettler, *Degrees of Inequality: How the Politics of Higher Education Sabotaged the American Dream* (New York: Basic Books, 2014), 2.

41. Kinser, *Main Street to Wall Street*, 28.

42. Ibid., 29.

43. Ibid., 66.

44. Ibid., 74.

45. Senate HELP Committee analysis of comprehensive student-level data provided by thirty for-profit education companies, including all publicly traded companies. Data from two companies were unusable due to compromised data integrity. Rates track students who enrolled between July 1, 2008, and June 30, 2009. For-profit education companies use different internal definitions of whether students are "active" or "withdrawn." The date a student is considered "withdrawn" varies from ten to ninety days from date of last attendance. Two companies provided amended data to properly account for students who had transferred within programs. Committee staff note that the data request instructed companies to provide a unique student identifier for each student, thus allowing accurate accounting of students who reentered or transferred programs within the school. The data set is current as of mid-2010; students who withdrew within the cohort period and reentered afterward are not counted. The for-profit model allows students to stop and easily reenroll, assuming they have no outstanding tuition balance with the school. It is unclear how many students who drop out within weeks or months of enrolling do in fact reenroll at a future date. Some students counted as withdrawals may have

transferred to other institutions. US Senate HELP Committee, *For Profit Higher Education*, 73–74.

46. College Board Advocacy and Policy Center, "Trends in College Pricing 2011," *College Board*, 2011, http://trends.collegeboard.org/sites/default/files/College_Pricing_2011.pdf, 13; US Senate HELP Committee, *For Profit Higher Education*.

47. *The Federal Investment in For-Profit Education: Are Students Succeeding? Hearing before the Senate Committee on Health, Education, Labor, and Pensions*, 111th Cong. (2010); US Senate HELP Committee, *For Profit Higher Education*, 95.

48. Matt Egan, "Government Ruling Sends Education Stocks Jumping," *FOX Business*, June 2, 2011, http://www.foxbusiness.com/industries/2011/06/02/for-profit-colleges-rally-as-government-test-looks-easy.

49. "Title IV Program Volume Reports," *Federal Student Aid: An Office of the U.S. Department of Education*, accessed July 12, 2012, http://federalstudentaid.ed.gov/datacenter/programmatic.html. Figures for 2000–2001 are calculated using data provided to the committee by the US Department of Education. Congress has taken steps to make college more accessible and affordable by committing $36 billion in mandatory Pell grant funding over the next ten years included in the Health Care and Education Reconciliation Act of 2010 and $17 billion in discretionary funding through the American Recovery and Reinvestment Act of 2009 and annual discretionary funding, which in fiscal year 2010 was $17.6 billion. For the 2009–2010 and 2010–2011 academic years, students attending year-round were also eligible to receive two Pell awards in one year, leading to a large increase in the total volume of Pell at many institutions in those years. Health Care and Education Reconciliation Act of 2010, Pub. L. No. 111–152, 124 Stat. 1029 (2010); American Recovery and Reinvestment Act of 2009, Pub. L. 111–5 (2009); US Senate HELP Committee, *For Profit Higher Education*, 25.

50. US Senate HELP Committee, *For Profit Higher Education*, 2.

51. Ibid., 81; see appendix 22.

2. HOOK, LINE, AND SINKER

1. Senate HELP Committee staff analysis of data provided by for-profit education companies. United States Senate Health, Education, Labor, and Pensions Committee (US Senate HELP Committee), *For Profit Higher Education: The Failure to Safeguard the Federal Investment and Ensure Student Success*, Majority Committee Staff Report and Accompanying Minority Committee Staff Views, July 30, 2012, 49, appendix 24.

2. ITT Educational Services, Inc., headquartered in Carmel, IN, enrolled approximately 88,000 students as of fall 2010. It operates ITT Technical Institute and Daniel Webster, with 145 campuses in 35 states and an online division. ITT offers primarily associate degree programs and small bachelor and master degree programs, with approximately 85 percent of ITT students enrolled in associate programs. US Senate HELP Committee, *For Profit Higher Education*, 21.

3. ITT, "Completed 2008 Performance Planning and Evaluation (PP&E) Form (ITT-00041048)," 2008. ITT states that this document is a draft. Below the corporate management level, directors of recruitment are judged based on the performance of the recruiters below them. An internal document from Vatterott Educational Centers, Inc., for example, shows that the recruiting director at a Vatterott campus was demoted for her department's failure to enroll enough students. Vatterott internal memorandum, "re: Transfer to Admissions Representative Position (VAT-02-15-00350)," October 2009; US Senate HELP Committee, *For Profit Higher Education*, 50.

4. Corinthian Colleges, Inc., headquartered in Santa Ana, CA, enrolled approximately 113,800 students as of fall 2010. Corinthian operates Everest, Heald College, and WyoTech, with more than 105 campuses in 25 states and online. It offers diploma and degree programs, with approximately 34 percent of students enrolled online and 64 percent enrolled in a nondegree program. US Senate HELP Committee, *For Profit Higher Education*, 20.

5. Corinthian College, "CCI Director of Admissions Operations Manual (CCi-00045638, at CCi-00045678-79)," 2008; US Senate HELP Committee, *For Profit Higher Education*, 51.

6. Education Management Corporation, headquartered in Pittsburgh, PA, enrolled approximately 158,000 students as of fall 2010. It operates Argosy University, the Art Institutes, Brown Mackie College, South University, and Western State University College of Law, with 107 campuses in 32 states and an online division. Education Management Corporation offers certificate, associate, bachelor, master, and doctoral programs, with approximately 25 percent of students enrolled exclusively online and nearly 50 percent of students enrolled in bachelor programs. Goldman Sachs owns 41.8 percent of EDMC. US Senate HELP Committee, *For Profit Higher Education*, 21.

7. EDMC internal e-mail, "re: FW: Conversion (EDMC-916-00034003) (Art Institute of Charlotte)," January 2008; US Senate HELP Committee, *For Profit Higher Education*, 51.

8. Corinthian Colleges, Inc., form 10-Q for period ending March 31, 2012; Corinthian Colleges, Inc., form 10-Q for the period ending December 31, 2011; Corinthian Colleges, Inc., form 10-Q for period ending September 31, 2012; Corinthian SEC quarterly filings. Churn can most easily be tracked for

public companies that report their quarterly enrollment numbers in SEC filings. US Senate HELP Committee, *For Profit Higher Education*, 77.

9. Thomas Bailey, Norena Badway, and Patricia J. Gumport, "For-Profit Higher Education and Community Colleges," *National Center for Postsecondary Improvement*, accessed April 27, 2013, http://www.stanford.edu/group/ncpi/documents/pdfs/forprofitandcc.pdf; US Senate HELP Committee, *For Profit Higher Education*, 31.

10. US Senate HELP Committee, *For Profit Higher Education*, 31. Senate HELP Committee staff analysis of IPEDS data.

11. "Report to the Congress on the Profitability of Credit Card Operations of Depository Institutions: Recent Trends in Credit Card Pricing," *Board of Governors of the Federal Reserve System*, June 2012, accessed July 5, 2013, http://www.federalreserve.gov/publications/other-reports/credit-card-profitability-2012-recent-trends-in-credit-card-pricing.htm; US Senate HELP Committee, *For Profit Higher Education*, 117.

12. Companies report spending on marketing and recruiting in different ways. In order to develop the most comprehensive estimate of spending on marketing and advertising as well as enrollment and recruiting for fiscal year 2009, committee staff used a combination of the annual 10-K statements of publicly traded companies, audited financial statements, and information produced pursuant to item number 1 of the second tranche in the committee document request of August 5, 2010 (see appendix 4). Form 10-K annual statements and financial statements were used wherever both marketing and recruiting expenses were broken out or where the two categories were combined ("marketing, promotion and selling"). US Senate HELP Committee, *For Profit Higher Education*, 81, appendix 22.

13. See, for example, Rasmussen, "Insertion Order (RAS00003280) ($37 per lead)," 2008; Rasmussen, "Advertising Agreement (RAS00003443) ($75 per lead)," 2008; Alta, "Lead Development, Maintaining High Conversion Rates (HELP-ALTA_000123) (Westwood College) ($150 per lead)," 2008.US Senate HELP Committee, *For Profit Higher Education*, 66.

14. Kaplan, Inc., headquartered in New York City, enrolled approximately 112,100 students as of fall 2010 and operates Kaplan Career Institute, College and University; Bauder College; CHI Institute; Concord Law School; Hesser College; Texas School of Business; and TESST College of Technology. With more than seventy campuses in twenty-one states and an online division, Kaplan offers certificate, associate, bachelor, and master degree programs, with approximately 60 percent of Kaplan students enrolled online. Kaplan is owned by the Washington Post Company. US Senate HELP Committee, *For Profit Higher Education*, 21.

15. Kaplan internal presentation, "Who Are Our Leads? (KHE 056401)," 2008; US Senate HELP Committee, *For Profit Higher Education*, 66.

16. US Senate HELP Committee, *For Profit Higher Education*, 66. See, for example, AcademixDirect, Inc., http://www.academixdirect.com ("100% of our business comes from the higher education market."); Lead2Class, *Higher Education Lead Generation Services*, http://www.lead2class.com ("Our approach to Internet advertising is highly targeted and designed to promote online education programs.").

17. See Josh Keller, "Online Search Ads Hijack Prospective Students, Former Employee Says," *Chronicle of Higher Education*, September 7, 2011, accessed May 3, 2012, http://chronicle.com/blogs/wiredcampus/online-search-ads-hijack-prospective-students-former-employee-says/33047 (Reporting that a former call center employee for Vantage Media recalled contacting "hundreds of students per day" and was "expected to keep students on the phone long enough to deliver three leads"). Lead-generation companies have been observed participating in Internet advertising campaigns that "falsely implied relationships with public colleges" in order to obtain prospective students' contact information for their for-profit clients. See also Josh Keller, "Colleges Fight Google Ads That Reroute Prospective Students," *Chronicle of Higher Education*, July 31, 2011, accessed May 3, 2012, http://chronicle.com/article/Colleges-Fight-Google-Ads-That/128414; US Senate HELP Committee, *For Profit Higher Education*, 66.

18. See "Online Business Administration Associate Degree Programs," *EarnMyDegree.com*, accessed December 15, 2011, www.earnmydegree.com/online-education/associate/business/business-administration.html; "Associate's in Business," *EarnMyDegree.com*, accessed May 3, 2012, www.earnmydegree.com/online-education/online-degrees/everest-university/business-associates-13.html; US Senate HELP Committee, *For Profit Higher Education*, 66.

19. Ibid.

20. "EducationConnection commercial," YouTube video, accessed July 15, 2012, http://www.youtube.com/watch?v=aDR28lIRGZw; US Senate HELP Committee, *For Profit Higher Education*, 67.

21. *For-Profit Schools: The Student Recruitment Experience, Hearing before the Senate Committee on Health, Education, Labor, and Pensions*, 111th Cong. (2010) (statement of Gregory Kutz, Managing Director, Office of Forensic Audits and Special Investigations, US Government Accountability Office); US Senate HELP Committee, *For Profit Higher Education*, 67.

22. Ibid.

23. ITT internal memorandum, "re: June Analysis 2007 (ITT-00025689)," June 2007. The company asserts that this document is not representative of the school's policies or procedures. See also Vatterott, "DDC Training (VAT-02-

14-03904)," March 2007; US Senate HELP Committee, *For Profit Higher Education*, 60.

24. ITT, "Increasing Your Scheduled to Conduct Ratio (ITT-00028362 at ITT-00028377)," 2008; US Senate HELP Committee, *For Profit Higher Education*, 60.

25. See, for example, *For-Profit Schools: The Student Recruitment Experience, Hearing Before the Senate Committee on Health, Education, Labor, and Pensions*, 111th Cong. (2010) (statement of Joshua Pruyn, Former Admissions Representative, Alta College, Inc., Denver, CO); US Senate HELP Committee, *For Profit Higher Education*, 60.

26. ITT, "Pain Funnel and Pain Puzzle (ITT-00010049)" (training materials prepared by Sandler Sales Institute), 2008. See also ITT, "ITT Technical Institute Questionnaire: Exhibit 3 (ITT-00010050)," 2008; Bridgepoint, "Psychology of a Student (BPI-HELP_00004019)," 2008; US Senate HELP Committee, *For Profit Higher Education*, 62.

27. ITT, "Completed Phoning Techniques Training Worksheet (ITT-00015566)," 2008. The company asserts that this document was created and used by only a few campus-level employees and never approved by the corporate office. US Senate HELP Committee, *For Profit Higher Education*, 61.

28. Kaplan, "Custom OBS and Quality Hybrid Job Aid Based on the Latest Undergraduate Outbound Script Published on April 2010 (KHE 096357)," April 2010; Kaplan, "Job Aid: Outbound with Rubric and OBS References Based on Undergraduate Script Published on July 8, 2009 (KHE 084935)," July 2009; US Senate HELP Committee, *For Profit Higher Education*, 62.

29. Kaplan, "Job Aid: Outbound with Rubric and OBS References Based on Undergraduate Script Published on July 8, 2009 (KHE 085294)," July 2009. Documents obtained by the committee contain multiple versions of the "ARTICHOKE" training. See, for example, Kaplan, "Custom OBS and Quality Hybrid Job Aid Based on the Latest Undergraduate Outbound Script Published on April 2010 (KHE 096357)," April 2010; US Senate HELP Committee, *For Profit Higher Education*, 63.

30. ITT, "Pain Funnel and Pain Puzzle (ITT-00010049)" (training materials prepared by Sandler Sales Institute), 2008. See also ITT, "ITT Technical Institute Questionnaire: Exhibit 3 (ITT-00010050)," 2008; Bridgepoint, "Psychology of a Student (BPI-HELP_00004019)," 2008; US Senate HELP Committee, *For Profit Higher Education*, 61.

31. Apollo Group, Inc., headquartered in Phoenix, AZ, enrolled approximately 470,800 students as of fall 2010 and operates University of Phoenix, the nation's largest for-profit college, and Western International University. Apollo Group offers bachelor, master, and doctoral programs, as well as an exclusively online associate program, in more than one hundred different fields. Founded

in 1978, it pioneered the modern for-profit education company. US Senate HELP Committee, *For Profit Higher Education*, 20.

32. Apollo, "Enrollment Counselor Guide: School of Advanced Studies (AGI0015231, at AGI0015333)" (University of Phoenix), 2007. The company states that this document is no longer used. US Senate HELP Committee, *For Profit Higher Education*, 64.

33. Ibid.

34. Career Education Corporation, headquartered in Schaumburg, IL, enrolled approximately 118,200 students as of fall 2010 and operates colleges under 11 brands, American InterContinental University, Briarcliff College, Brooke Institute, Brown College, Collins College, Colorado Technical University, Harrington College of Design, International Academy of Design and Technology, Le Cordon Bleu, Missouri College, and Sanford-Brown, with 83 campuses and 4 online divisions. It offers certificates as well as associate, bachelor, master, and doctoral degree programs, with nearly 40 percent of students enrolled online. US Senate HELP Committee, *For Profit Higher Education*, 20.

35. Career Education Corporation, "Telephone Techniques (CEC000014470)"; US Senate HELP Committee, *For Profit Higher Education*, 64.

36. Bridgepoint, "Creating Urgency (BPI-HELP_00005972)"; US Senate HELP Committee, *For Profit Higher Education*, 64.

37. Kaplan internal record, "Record of Student's Family's Letter of Complaint (KHE 0038287)," July 2006; US Senate HELP Committee, *For Profit Higher Education*, 113.

38. Laura Brozek, former executive manager of recruiting at ITT, letter, June 24, 2012; US Senate HELP Committee, *For Profit Higher Education*, 61.

3. VETERANS IN THE CROSSHAIRS

1. The Higher Education Amendments of 1992 (PL 102-325, July 23, 1992) amended subsection 481(b) paragraph 6 of the Higher Education Act of 1965 [20 USC 1088(b)] to introduce the 85/15 rule effective October 1, 1992. "90/10 Rule," *FinAid*, 2015, http://www.finaid.org/loans/90-10-rule.phtml.

2. The Higher Education Amendments of 1998 (PL 105-244, October 7, 1998) moved the language defining the 85/15 rule to section 102(b)(1)(F) of the Higher Education Act of 1965 [20 USC 1002(b)(1)(F)] and substituted "10 percent" for "15 percent" and "Title IV" for "this title," effective October 1, 1998. "90/10 Rule."

3. The Higher Education Act of 1965 section 487(a) [20 USC 1094(a)(24)] effective August 14, 2008. "90/10 Rule."

4. "Watch now: An ITT Tech special salute to veterans," YouTube video, posted by "ITT Technical Institute," November 9, 2012, accessed May 29, 2013, http://www.youtube.com/watch?v=6BNMPujU3dY.

5. Kaplan internal presentation, "Kaplan Military University (KHE 267362)," 2009. It is unclear whether the company invested these resources in their military efforts given that the company received comparably little post-9/11 GI bill funds in the years following the presentation. United States Senate Health, Education, Labor, and Pensions Committee (US Senate HELP Committee), *For Profit Higher Education: The Failure to Safeguard the Federal Investment and Ensure Student Success*, Majority Committee Staff Report and Accompanying Minority Committee Staff Views, July 30, 2012, 68.

6. Ibid.

7. ITT internal e-mail, "fw:Stifel:Education-Summary from the CCME Conference Kickoff (ITT-00140384)"; U.S. Senate HELP Committee, *For Profit Higher Education*, 68.

8. "Watch now."

9. A review of documents provided to the committee shows that Quin-Street provided lead-generation services to Anthem Education Group; Apollo Group, Inc.; Capella Education Company; Concorde Career Colleges, Inc.; DeVry, Inc.; ECPI Colleges, Inc.; National American University Holdings, Inc.; TUI Learning LLC; Universal Technical Institute, Inc.; and Walden University. The following is the full list of QuinStreet-owned lead-generator sites: ArmyStudyGuide.com, ArmyToolbag.com, GIBenefits.com, GIBill.com, GI-BillAmerica.com, GruntsMilitary.com, Military-Net.com, MilitaryConnections.com, MilitaryGIBill.com, MilitaryPay.com, NavyStoreKeeper.com, US-Army-Info.com, and VNIS.com. See also "Connecting Customers to You," *QuinStreet*, accessed May 3, 2013, http://quinstreet.com/what_we_do; Army "Tools for Army Leaders," *ArmyToolbag*, http://www.armytoolbag.com; US Senate HELP Committee, *For Profit Higher Education*, 68.

10. See "WEAMS Public," *US Department of Veterans Affairs*, accessed May 3, 2012, http://inquiry.vba.va.gov/weamspub/searchInst.do#content-area; US Senate HELP Committee, *For Profit Higher Education*, 69.

11. Office of the Attorney General, "Attorney General Conway Announces Win for Veterans against Predatory Practices," news release, June 27, 2012, accessed May 3, 2013, http://migration.kentucky.gov/Newsroom/ag/quinstreetavc.htm.

12. US Senate HELP Committee, *For Profit Higher Education*, 69. See "Welcome to the GI Bill Web Site," *US Department of Veterans Affairs*, http://www.gibill.va.gov.

13. Daniel Golden, "Marine Can't Recall His Lessons at For-Profit College (Update 2)," *Bloomberg*, December 15, 2009, accessed May 3, 2013, http://www.bloomberg.com/apps/news?pid=newsarchive&sid=al8HttoCG.ps; US Senate HELP Committee, *For Profit Higher Education*, 69.

14. Kaplan, "Military Training (KHE 267268)," 2010. Kaplan states that this document does not reflect a training program approved or implemented by Kaplan or Kaplan's approach to enrollment of military personnel. US Senate HELP Committee, *For Profit Higher Education*, 69.

15. Grand Canyon University, "re: RE: Pizza Receipt (GCUHELP 019907)," April 2010. Grand Canyon Education, Inc. ("Grand Canyon") is a publicly traded for-profit higher education company that enrolled 42,300 students as of 2010 and is based in Phoenix, AZ. US Senate HELP Committee, *For Profit Higher Education*, 70.

16. US Senate HELP Committee, *For Profit Higher Education*, 28. The University of Maryland system and the University of Texas system are the two nonprofit recipients of post-9/11 GI bill funds, largely due to their close proximity to a concentration of military bases.

17. Ibid.

18. Ibid.

19. Ibid.

20. "US Department of Defense Instruction, Voluntary Education Programs, Number 1322.25," *Defense Technical Information Center*, March 15, 2011, accessed May 24, 2012, http://www.dtic.mil/whs/directives/corres/pdf/132225p.pdf. Provides $250 per semester credit hour, or $166 per quarter credit hour, depending on the institution's academic calendar. US Senate HELP Committee, *For Profit Higher Education*, 30.

21. See US Senate HELP Committee, *For Profit Higher Education*, 30, appendix 12. Senate HELP Committee staff analysis of data provided by the Department of Defense.

22. "MyCAA Fact Sheet," *Department of Defense*, accessed July 1, 2012, http://www.militaryhomefront.dod.mil/mycaa/FactSheet; US Senate HELP Committee, *For Profit Higher Education*, 30.

23. See US Senate HELP Committee, *For Profit Higher Education*, 30, appendix 12. Senate HELP Committee staff analysis of data provided by the Department of Defense.

24. Ibid. Senate HELP Committee staff analysis of data provided by the Department of Defense.

25. See H.R. Rep. No. 1943, 82nd Cong. (1952); US Senate HELP Committee, *For Profit Higher Education*, 147.

26. "Benefiting Whom? For-Profit Education Companies and the Growth of Military Education Benefits," *Hearing Before the Subcommittee on Federal*

Financial Management, Government Information, Federal Services and International Security, U.S. Senate Committee on Homeland Security and Governmental Affairs (September 22, 2011) (statement of Hollister Petraeus, Head of the Office of Servicemember Affairs at the Consumer Financial Protection Bureau); US Senate HELP Committee, *For Profit Higher Education*, 147.

27. Bridgepoint Education, Inc., headquartered in San Diego, CA, enrolled approximately 77,200 students as of fall 2010 and operates Ashford University and University of the Rockies with two campuses and 99 percent of students enrolled exclusively online. It offers bachelor and associate degrees through Ashford University and master and doctoral degrees through University of the Rockies. The private equity firm Warburg Pincus owns 67.4 percent of the company. US Senate HELP Committee, *For Profit Higher Education*, 20.

28. Bridgepoint CEO Andrew Clark presentation to Deutsche Bank Conference, February 8, 2010; US Senate HELP Committee, *For Profit Higher Education*, 147.

29. Ibid.

30. Consultant memorandum, "EDMC-916-000228224," July 2010. The consultant's website lists a number of colleges, including Corinthian, Des Moines Area Community College, George Mason, and University of North Texas, as clients, but EDMC was never a client of Strategic Partnerships. See "Clients," *Strategic Partnerships LLC*, accessed June 28, 2012, http://strategic-partnershipsllc.com/clients.cfm; US Senate HELP Committee, *For Profit Higher Education*, 148.

31. Ibid.

32. Kaplan internal e-mail, "re: FW: KU 90/10 Issue (KHE 211344)," November 2009; US Senate HELP Committee, *For Profit Higher Education*, 148.

33. Senate HELP Committee staff analysis of "Title IV Program Volume Reports for Kaplan," *US Department of Education, Federal Student Aid Data Center*, 2009, http://federalstudentaid.ed.gov/datacenter/programmatic.html; US Senate HELP Committee, *For Profit Higher Education*, 148.

34. "Senator Harkin and Senator Carper Unveil New Data on Post-9/11 G.I. Bill Benefits and For Profit Colleges," video, http://harkin.senate.gov/help/video_press.cfm; US Senate HELP Committee, *For Profit Higher Education*, 70.

35. Ibid.

36. Ibid.

37. Hollister K. Petraeus, "For-Profit Colleges, Vulnerable G.I.'s," *New York Times*, September 21, 2011, accessed May 24, 2012, http://www.nytimes.com/2011/09/22/opinion/for-profit-colleges-vulnerable-gis.html; US Senate HELP Committee, *For Profit Higher Education*, 71.

4. FILLING THE GAP OR FILLING SEATS?

1. "Let's Get to Work, America," YouTube video, posted by University of Phoenix, accessed June 6, 2013, http://www.youtube.com/watch?v=BclAhAU40ss.

2. "Mission and Purpose," *University of Phoenix*, accessed June 6, 2013, http://www.phoenix.edu/about_us/about_university_of_phoenix/mission_and_purpose.html.

3. "The Ashford Mission," *Ashford University*, accessed June 6, 2013, http://www.ashford.edu/about/ashford_mission.htm.

4. DeVry bus stop ad, http://images.greatergreaterwashington.org/images/200903/devry.jpg (on file with the Senate HELP Committee); United States Senate Health, Education, Labor, and Pensions Committee (US Senate HELP Committee), *For Profit Higher Education: The Failure to Safeguard the Federal Investment and Ensure Student Success*, Majority Committee Staff Report and Accompanying Minority Committee Staff Views, July 30, 2012, 98.

5. US Senate HELP Committee, *For Profit Higher Education*, 97, appendix 24. TUI and Walden did not provide information for 2010. Additionally, TUI, Chancellor, and Henley Putnam were not in existence for the entire period, and CEC provided only one year of information.

6. Ibid.

7. Ibid.

8. Ibid.

9. Ibid.

10. "Mission and Purpose," *University of Phoenix*.

11. Bridgepoint student e-mail, "re: This is my formal complaint (BPI-HELP_00027543)," July 2008; US Senate HELP Committee, *For Profit Higher Education*, 97.

12. ITT student complaint, "Student Letter of Complaint (ITT-00004357)," June 2006; US Senate HELP Committee, *For Profit Higher Education*, 97.

13. US Senate HELP Committee, *For Profit Higher Education*, 20.

14. US Senate HELP Committee, *For Profit Higher Education*, 74, "For-Profit Education Companies with the Highest Associate Degree Withdrawal Rates" table.

15. GAO employees attempted to enroll at fifteen different institutions using fictitious (and unverifiable) proofs of graduation from a high school or its equivalent. Only three of the fifteen schools declined or rescinded the students' admissions as a result of those unverifiable credentials, while the other twelve institutions allowed admission. See US Government Accountability Office, *For Profit Schools: Experiences of Undercover Students Enrolled in Online Classes at Selected Colleges*, report to the chairman, Committee on

Health, Education, Labor, and Pensions, October 2011, http://www.gao.gov/assets/590/586456.pdf [hereafter GAO II]; US Senate HELP Committee, *For Profit Higher Education*, 89.

16. GAO investigation documentation, "History of Electronic Messages between GAO Investigator and Online Intro to Computer Instructor (GAOHQ-4750764)," January 2011; GAO investigation documentation, "Week Two Class Discussion, Instructions and Student Comments (DALLAS-334889)," May 2011; GAO investigation documentation, "ITT Technical Institute Discussion Forum Summary Page (HQ-4643279)," December 2011. See, for example, GAO investigation documentation, "Title: TB 141 Week 2 Quiz (HQ-4628843)," 2011; GAO investigation documentation, "Record of Analysis: Rasmussen—IB—Week 7 Quiz (HQ-4687765)," February 2011; US Senate HELP Committee, *For Profit Higher Education*, 89.

17. GAO investigation documentation, "History of Electronic Messages between GAO Investigator and Online Intro to Computer Instructor (GAOHQ-4750764)," January 2011; GAO investigation documentation, "Week Two Class Discussion, Instructions and Student Comments (DALLAS-334889)," May 2011; GAO investigation documentation, "ITT Technical Institute Discussion Forum Summary Page (HQ-4643279)," December 2011; GAO investigation documentation, "Title: TB 141 Week 2 Quiz (HQ-4628843)," 2011; GAO investigation documentation, "Record of Analysis: Rasmussen—IB—Week 7 Quiz (HQ-4687765)," February 2011; GAO investigation documentation, "The Gross Domestic Product (HQ-4600689)," 2011; GAO investigation documentation, "A SWOT Analysis for Online Learning (HQ-4631902)," 2011; US Senate HELP Committee, *For Profit Higher Education*, 89.

18. GAO investigation documentation, "Title: TB 141 Week 2 Quiz (HQ-4628843)," 2011; US Senate HELP Committee, *For Profit Higher Education*, 89.

19. GAO II, "Table 1: Federal Financial Aid and Out-of-Pocket Costs of Undercover Student Attendance at 15 For-Profit Colleges"; US Senate HELP Committee, *For Profit Higher Education*, 90.

20. Ibid.

21. GAO investigation documentation, "Title: TB 141 Week 2 Quiz (HQ-4628843)," 2011; US Senate HELP Committee, *For Profit Higher Education*, 89.

22. ITT Educational Services, "Letter from Better Business Bureau Regarding a Student Complaint (ITT-00009785)," July 2010; US Senate HELP Committee, *For Profit Higher Education*, 93.

23. ITT Educational Services, "Completed Student Comment/Complaint Report (ITT-00003876)," August 2006; US Senate HELP Committee, *For Profit Higher Education*, 93.

24. Herzing, Inc., headquartered in Milwaukee, WI, enrolled approximately 8,200 students as of fall 2010 and operates eleven campuses in eight states and online. It offers associate, bachelor, and online master degree programs in business management, electronics, health care, graphic design, and public safety. US Senate HELP Committee, *For Profit Higher Education*, 23.

25. Herzing student e-mail, "Student Letter of Complaint (HP000002321)," November 2009; US Senate HELP Committee, *For Profit Higher Education*, 93.

26. Universal Technical Institute, Inc., headquartered in Scottsdale, AZ, enrolled approximately 21,000 students as of fall 2010 and operates Universal Technical Institute, Motorcycle Mechanics Institute, Marine Mechanics Institute, and NASCAR Technical Institute, with no online division. It offers diploma and associate degree programs in mechanical and automotive fields. US Senate HELP Committee, *For Profit Higher Education*, 21.

27. UTI internal e-mail, "re: FW: Course 2 ESI full report (UTI-C-001040, at UTI-C-001041)," October 2007; US Senate HELP Committee, *For Profit Higher Education*, 93.

28. Kaplan, "Document Describing Complaint from a HVAC Student (KHE 0038727)," August 2009; US Senate HELP Committee, *For Profit Higher Education*, 93.

29. GAO investigation documentation, "Career Point College, Introduction to Computers Syllabus and Course Outline (GAOHQ-4662274)," August 2010; US Senate HELP Committee, *For Profit Higher Education*, 91.

30. GAO investigation documentation, "History of Electronic Messages between GAO Investigator and Online Intro to Computer Instructor (GAOHQ-4750764)," January 2011; US Senate HELP Committee, *For Profit Higher Education*, 92.

31. Kaplan internal document, "Student Complaint Record (KHE 0039787)," October 2008; US Senate HELP Committee, *For Profit Higher Education*, 97.

32. Ibid.

33. Herzing student correspondence, "re: Herzing University at Birmingham, AL (HP000002286)," May 2009; US Senate HELP Committee, *For Profit Higher Education*, 97.

34. "Mission and Purpose," *University of Phoenix*.

35. UTI internal e-mail, "re: FW; (UTI-C-000492)," August 2008. UTI was not one of the institutions investigated by GAO II. US Senate HELP Committee, *For Profit Higher Education*, 92.

36. "Our Mission," *Kaplan University*, accessed June 6, 2013, http://www.kaplanuniversity.edu/about/about-kaplan-university.aspx.

37. While the identity of individual companies were not made public at the time of the release of the GAO report "For-Profit Schools: Experiences of Undercover Students Enrolled in Online Classes at Selected Colleges," the information was provided to the committee. The undercover GAO staff enrolled in the following schools: Community Care College, Bridgepoint-owned Ashford University, Kaplan University, Career Point College, CEC-owned International Academy of Design and Technology, Rasmussen College, Corinthian-owned Everest College, Newport Business Institute, Pinnacle Career Institute, ITT, Fortis College, and Trumbell Business College. The three schools that did not permit GAO to enroll were University of Phoenix, DeVry, and Anthem. ITT was school number 10 in the GAO report, Rasmussen was school number 6, and Corinthian-owned Everest College was school number 7. US Senate HELP Committee, *For Profit Higher Education*, 90.

38. Another agent submitted a single partially plagiarized assignment at a sixth school, Community Care College, and received partial credit for that assignment in accordance with the school's policies. See GAO II at 12; US Senate HELP Committee, *For Profit Higher Education*, 90.

39. Ibid.

40. US Senate HELP Committee, *For Profit Higher Education*, 98.

41. US Senate HELP Committee staff analysis of documents produced by the companies. In Apollo's response, found in appendix 6, the company, for the first time, stated to the committee that it utilizes a third-party provider to "accelerate the delivery of career services to University of Phoenix students." US Senate HELP Committee, *For Profit Higher Education*, 98, appendixes 7 and 24.

42. US Senate HELP Committee staff analysis of documents produced by the University of Phoenix. US Senate HELP Committee, *For Profit Higher Education*, 98.

43. *The Federal Investment in For-Profit Education: Are Students Succeeding? Hearing before the Senate Committee on Health, Education, Labor, and Pensions*, 111th Cong. (2010) (statement of Kathleen A. Bittel, Acme, PA); US Senate HELP Committee, *For Profit Higher Education*, 98.

44. Ibid.

45. Concorde external correspondence, "Notification of Student Complaint Submitted to the Better Business Bureau (CCC000110342)," December 2009 US Senate HELP Committee, *For Profit Higher Education*, 99.

46. Paul Scazillo, former instructor at UEI College, letter to Chairman Tom Harkin, July 7, 2010. UEI is not one of the thirty for-profit higher education companies that received a document request from the committee during its investigation. US Senate HELP Committee, *For Profit Higher Education*, 99.

5. COOKING THE BOOKS

1. *The Federal Investment in For-Profit Education: Are Students Succeeding? Hearing before the Senate Committee on Health, Education, Labor, and Pensions*, 111th Cong. (2010) (statement of Kathleen A. Bittel, Acme, PA); United States Senate Health, Education, Labor, and Pensions Committee (US Senate HELP Committee), *For Profit Higher Education: The Failure to Safeguard the Federal Investment and Ensure Student Success*, Majority Committee Staff Report and Accompanying Minority Committee Staff Views, July 30, 2012, 100.

2. Ibid.

3. Ibid.

4. Kaplan internal e-mail, "re: Re: MOS and MA Graduates (KHE279471)," May 2010; US Senate HELP Committee, *For Profit Higher Education*, 100.

5. *Federal Investment* (Bittel); US Senate HELP Committee, *For Profit Higher Education*, 101.

6. ITT internal document, "Career Services Graduate Employment Definitions CS-2 (ITT-00065475)."; US Senate HELP Committee, *For Profit Higher Education*, 101.

7. ITT internal document, "FAQs on Employment Classification (ITT-00065499, at ITT-00065501)," 2010; US Senate HELP Committee, *For Profit Higher Education*, 101.

8. Mark Greenblatt, "Whistle-Blower: For-Profit College Operator Allegedly Inflates Job Placement Rates," *ABC News*, November 26, 2012, accessed June 14, 2013, http://abcnews.go.com/US/whistle-blower-profit-college-operator-allegedly-inflates-job/story?id=17810902#.Ub6H698o6Uk.

9. Ibid.

10. Ibid.

11. Ibid.

12. Ibid.

13. Ibid.

14. Ibid.

15. Ibid.

16. Ibid.

17. Ibid.

18. Ibid.

19. Ibid.

20. Ibid.

21. National Conference of Bar Examiners and American Bar Association Section of Legal Education and Admissions to the Bar, "Comprehensive Guide

to Bar Admission Requirements 2012," *National Conference of Bar Examiners*, 2012, accessed May 15, 2012, http://www.ncbex.org/assets/media_files/Comp-Guide/2012CompGuide.pdf; US Senate HELP Committee, *For Profit Higher Education*, 102.

22. S. David Young, "Occupational Licensing," *Library of Economics and Liberty*, 2002, accessed June 20, 2013, http://www.econlib.org/library/Enc1/OccupationalLicensing.html#abouttheauthor.

23. US Senate HELP Committee, *For Profit Higher Education*, 102.

24. Ibid.

25. *Emerging Risk? Federal Spending on For-Profit Education Hearing Before the Senate Committee on Health, Education, Labor, and Pensions*, 111th Cong. (2010) (statement of Yasmine Issa, Yonkers, NY); US Senate HELP Committee, *For Profit Higher Education*, 103.

26. Ibid.

27. Ibid. ARDMS is not itself a programmatic accrediting agency, rather it allows students to sit for examination who graduate from programs accredited by the Commission on Accreditation of Allied Health Education Programs (CAAHEP). The program Ms. Issa attended is not accredited by CAAHEP.

28. *Emerging Risk?* (Issa); US Senate HELP Committee, *For Profit Higher Education*, 103.

29. *Drowning in Debt: Financial Outcomes of Students at For-Profit Colleges, Hearing before the Senate Committee on Health, Education, Labor, and Pensions*, 111th Cong. (2011) (statement of Eric Schmitt, Hampton, IA). See also Eric Schmitt, e-mail to the Senate Committee on Health, Education, Labor, and Pensions (US Senate HELP Committee), March 28, 2011 (on file with committee); US Senate HELP Committee, *For Profit Higher Education*, 104.

30. *Federal Investment* (Bittel); US Senate HELP Committee, *For Profit Higher Education*, 100.

31. *Drowning in Debt* (Schmitt). See also Schmitt, e-mail to US Senate HELP Committee, March 28, 2011. The company states that the initial conversation with the dean, according to Mr. Schmitt's testimony, occurred in the second year of his associate degree program when law school was no more than a thought on the horizon. The company also states that Mr. Schmitt never applied to Concord Law School, and if he had, he would have immediately learned that he would not be eligible to sit for the Iowa bar exam. US Senate HELP Committee, *For Profit Higher Education*, 104.

32. Brian Burnsed, "Online Law Schools Have Yet to Pass the Bar," *US News Education: Online Education*, June 20, 2012.

33. US Senate HELP Committee, *For Profit Higher Education*, table 2, 74.

34. *Bridgepoint Education, Inc.: A Case Study in For-Profit Education and Oversight, Hearing before the Senate Committee on Health, Education, Labor, and Pensions*, 112th Cong. (2011) (Arlie Thoreson Willems, Ph.D., Administrative Consultant for Practitioner Preparation, Iowa Department of Education, retired); US Senate HELP Committee, *For Profit Higher Education*, 104.

35. Ibid.

36. US Senate HELP Committee, *For Profit Higher Education*, 20.

37. *Bridgepoint Education, Inc.* (Willems); US Senate HELP Committee, *For Profit Higher Education*, 104. Although Ashford's brick-and-mortar education programs do qualify graduates for a teaching credential, the institution's online education programs do not meet the state's Department of Education standards. Therefore, graduates from the online program cannot use their degrees to qualify for a teaching credential in Iowa. Further, more than 99 percent of Ashford's students are online-only students. See, chapter on Bridgepoint, infra.

38. Bridgepoint, "Formal Grievance Submission Form and Attachments (BPI-HELP_00026808)," August 2010; US Senate HELP Committee, *For Profit Higher Education*, 105.

39. Kaplan, "Record of Student Complaint and Follow-Up (KHE0038613)," August 2007; US Senate HELP Committee, *For Profit Higher Education*, 105.

6. LENDING LIES

1. United States Senate Health, Education, Labor, and Pensions Committee (US Senate HELP Committee), *For Profit Higher Education: The Failure to Safeguard the Federal Investment and Ensure Student Success*, Majority Committee Staff Report and Accompanying Minority Committee Staff Views, July 30, 2012, 14.

2. Ibid., figure 1, 36. See appendix 14 for a complete list of programs and tuition.

3. Ibid.

4. Ibid.

5. Ibid., figure 1, 37. See appendix 14 for a complete list of programs and tuition.

6. Ibid.

7. Ibid.

8. Ibid.

9. Ibid., 37.

10. Ibid.

11. Higher Education Amendments of 1972, Pub. L. No. 92-318, 86 Stat. 235 (1972); College Board Advocacy and Policy Center, "Trends in College Pricing 2011," *College Board*, 2011, http://trends.collegeboard.org/sites/default/files/College_Pricing_2011.pdf, 13; US Senate HELP Committee, *For Profit Higher Education*, 39.

12. David J. Deming, Claudia Goldin, and Lawrance F. Katz, "The For-Profit Postsecondary School Sector: Nimble Critters or Agile Predators?" *Journal of Economic Perspectives* 26, no. 1 (Winter 2012), 139–64, http://www.frbatlanta.org/documents/news/conferences/11employment_education_demming.pdf; US Senate HELP Committee, *For Profit Higher Education*, 39.

13. US Senate HELP Committee, *For Profit Higher Education*, 40.

14. Alta, "Pricing Manager Business Case (HELP-ALTA-000153, at HELP-ALTA-000159)," February 2009; US Senate HELP Committee, *For Profit Higher Education*, 41.

15. Deming, Goldin, and Katz, "For-Profit Postsecondary School Sector"; US Senate HELP Committee, *For Profit Higher Education*, 40.

16. US Senate HELP Committee, *For Profit Higher Education*, 40.

17. Bridgepoint internal e-mail, "re: Re: MAJOR ISSUE (BPI-HELP_00048618, at BPI-HELP_00048619)," February 2010; US Senate HELP Committee, *For Profit Higher Education*, 40.

18. Ibid.

19. "Tuition and Fees," *Ashford University*, accessed May 3, 2012, http://www.ashford.edu/admissions/online_tuition_fees.htm; US Senate HELP Committee, *For Profit Higher Education*, 46.

20. See "Course Catalog Addendum Effective 08/01/12," *Westwood*, accessed July 1, 2012, http://www.westwood.edu/~/media/Files/files/pdf/catalogs/wco_addendum.ashx. See also Westwood internal document, "Draft Tuition Pricing Table (WP000003947)," 2008; Westwood internal document, "Draft Tuition Pricing (WP000003948)," 2008; Westwood internal presentation, "Marketing Presentation on Tuition Pricing (WP000004111)," 2009; Westwood internal presentation, "Marketing Presentation on Tuition Pricing (WP000004381)," 2009; US Senate HELP Committee, *For Profit Higher Education*, 46.

21. US Senate HELP Committee, *For Profit Higher Education*, 45. Rasmussen Colleges, Inc. ("Rasmussen"), is a for-profit higher-education company that enrolled 17,090 students as of fall 2010 and is based in Minnetonka, MN.

22. "Tuition at Rasmussen College," *Rasmussen*, accessed May 2, 2012, www.rasmussen.edu/tuition; US Senate HELP Committee, *For Profit Higher Education*, 45.

23. "Search Results for Tuition," *Rasmussen*, accessed May 22, 2012, www.rasmussen.edu/search?s=tuition&x=0&y=0; US Senate HELP Committee, *For Profit Higher Education*, 45.

24. "Tuition, Fees, and Median Loan Debt Disclosure," *Colorado Technical University*, accessed May 3, 2012, http://www.coloradotech.edu/Disclosures/~/media/Disclosures/CTU/Colorado-Springs/Colorado-Technical-University-Colorado-Springs-010148-00-Tuition-Debt-Disclosure.ashx. Colorado Technical University is a brand operated by Career Education Corporation ("CEC"), a publicly traded for-profit higher-education company that enrolled 118,205 students as of fall 2010 and is based in Schaumburg, IL. US Senate HELP Committee, *For Profit Higher Education*, 46.

25. Ibid.

26. While the disclosure appears to be in compliance with the regulation, if the required credit hours are multiplied by the current cost per credit hour, the cost is significantly higher than the disclosure suggests.

27. Doug Lederman, "The Credit Crunch Takes a Toll," *Inside Higher Ed*, January 23, 2008, accessed May 9, 2012, http://www.insidehighered.com/news/2008/01/23/credit; US Senate HELP Committee, *For Profit Higher Education*, 117.

28. Higher Education Act: Revenue Generated from Institutional Aid (Sec. 668.28). The provision reads, "With regard to a loan made by a third party to a student at an institution, in the normal course, the proceeds of the loan would be credited to the student's account, and the amount credited that paid for tuition and fees not covered by Title IV, HEA aid would count as non-Title IV, HEA revenue in the 90/10 calculation."

29. US Department of Education, "General GSA Participation Requirements," *Federal Student Aid Handbook* 2 (March 2009), accessed May 11, 2012, http://ifap.ed.gov/fsahandbook/attachments/0910FSAHbk-Vol2Ch3GenRequirements.pdf, 32; US Senate HELP Committee, *For Profit Higher Education*, 145.

30. US Senate HELP Committee, *For Profit Higher Education*, "Company Profiles: ITT Education Services Inc.," 526.

31. Ibid.

32. Ibid.

33. Ibid.

34. ITT Educational Services, "Private Education Loan Application and Solicitation Disclosure by Liberty Bank (ITT-00080791)," 2009; US Senate HELP Committee, *For Profit Higher Education*, "Company Profiles: ITT Education Services Inc.," 526.

35. US Senate HELP Committee, *For Profit Higher Education*, 117. Note that in 2010 Corinthian lowered its rate to 6.8 percent.

36. Ibid., "Institutional Loan Interest Rates by Company in 2009" table, 117.

37. Ibid.

38. Kaplan internal e-mail, "re: RE: KC Loan Default Assumption/[Redacted] (KHE 137576)," April 2009; US Senate HELP Committee, *For Profit Higher Education*, 118.

39. Ibid.

40. US Senate HELP Committee, *For Profit Higher Education*, "Institutional Loan Program Expected Student Default Rates by Company in 2009" table, 118.

41. Senate HELP Committee staff analysis of US Department of Education Trial Cohort Default Rates fiscal years 2005–2008, http://federalstudentaid.ed.gov/datacenter/cohort.html. Default rates calculated by cumulating the number of students entered into repayment and default by sector. US Senate HELP Committee, *For Profit Higher Education*, 114.

42. *Drowning in Debt: Financial Outcomes of Students at For-Profit Colleges Hearing before the Senate Committee on Health, Education, Labor, and Pensions*, 112th Cong. (2011) (statement of Sandy Baum, Policy Analyst, the College Board, and Senior Fellow, George Washington University School of Education and Human Development), "Share of Students Borrowing by Sector in 2009" table; US Senate HELP Committee, *For Profit Higher Education*, 112.

43. Herzing internal e-mail, "re: Tuition Increase Recommendations (HP000006785)," November 2009. Herzing, Inc. ("Herzing"), is a for-profit higher-education company that enrolled 8,253 students as of 2010 and is based in Milwaukee, WI. US Senate HELP Committee, *For Profit Higher Education*, 43.

44. Herzing internal e-mail, "re: Tuition (HP000005730, at HP000005730)," November 2009; US Senate HELP Committee, *For Profit Higher Education*, 43.

45. See, for example, Herzing, "Tuition Price Increases between 2009–10 (HP000005259)," 2010; US Senate HELP Committee, *For Profit Higher Education*, 43.

46. Kaplan internal e-mail, "re: RE: Tuition Discussion with Campus Presidents (KHE 178035, at KHE 178035)," December 2009; US Senate HELP Committee, *For Profit Higher Education*, 43.

47. Apollo internal e-mail, "re: RE: GP (AGI0045758) (University of Phoenix)," October 2008; US Senate HELP Committee, *For Profit Higher Education*, 44.

48. Senate HELP Committee analysis of comprehensive student-level data provided by thirty for-profit education companies, including all publicly traded

companies. Data from two companies were unusable due to compromised data integrity. Rates track students who enrolled between July 1, 2008, and June 30, 2009. For-profit education companies use different internal definitions of whether students are "active" or "withdrawn." The date a student is considered "withdrawn" varies from ten to ninety days from date of last attendance. US Senate HELP Committee, *For Profit Higher Education*, 73.

49. US Senate HELP Committee, *For Profit Higher Education*, "Status of Students Enrolled in For-Profit Education Companies in 2008–9 as of 2010" table, 74.

50. US Senate HELP Committee, *For Profit Higher Education*, "For-Profit Education Companies with the Highest Associate Degree Withdrawal Rates" table, 74.

51. Ibid.

52. Ibid.

7. DREAMS DESTROYED

1. United States Senate Health, Education, Labor, and Pensions Committee (US Senate HELP Committee), *For Profit Higher Education: The Failure to Safeguard the Federal Investment and Ensure Student Success*, Majority Committee Staff Report and Accompanying Minority Committee Staff Views, July 30, 2012, 151. Under 34 CFR 668.187(a), a school loses eligibility for federal loans if the cohort default rate is greater than 40 percent in a single year or if the cohort default rate (CDR) is greater than 25 percent for each of the three most recent years. An institution's CDR is the percentage of the institution's former student borrowers who entered repayment on a federal student loan during the relevant cohort year who defaulted before the end of the next government fiscal year following the cohort year. The government fiscal year begins on October 1. Therefore, for example, a student who leaves school in August 2010 would enter repayment after the six-month grace period in February 2011. This student would be included in the school's fiscal year 2011 CDR. If the student defaults any time before the start of fiscal year 2013 on October 1, 2012, then the student would be counted as a "defaulter" under the current two-year window. Under the three-year window, if the student defaults any time before October 1, 2013, the student would be counted as a "defaulter." Under the direct loan program, default is defined as 360 days of delinquency.

2. Corinthian Colleges, Inc., "Form 8-K Filed February 28, 2012"; US Senate HELP Committee, *For Profit Higher Education*, table 1, "Corinthian Colleges Institutions by Default Rate," 158.

3. Senate HELP Committee staff analysis of US Department of Education Trial Cohort Default Rates fiscal years 2005–2008, http://federalstudentaid.ed.gov/datacenter/cohort.html. In March 2012, Corinthian announced that its 2009 three-year default rate had fallen by 7.3 percent to 28.8 percent. US Senate HELP Committee, *For Profit Higher Education*, 116.

4. Ibid.

5. Corinthian Colleges, Inc., "Form 8-K. Filed March 5, 2012"; US Senate HELP Committee, *For Profit Higher Education*, 158.

6. US Department of Education, "First Official Three-Year Student Loan Default Rates," September 28, 2012.

7. "Deferment and Forbearance," *Federal Student Aid, Office of the US Department of Education*, accessed July 4, 2013, http://studentaid.ed.gov/repay-loans/deferment-forbearance.

8. US Senate HELP Committee, *For Profit Higher Education*, 153.

9. Ibid., 155. They are Apollo, Bridgepoint, Capella, Corinthian, DeVry, EDMC, ITT, Kaplan, Lincoln, National American, Rasmussen, and Strayer.

10. Ibid.

11. ITT internal record, "Cohort Default Management Solutions Executive Dashboard: Table of Key Performance Indicators (ITT-00002316)," August 2010; Bridgepoint internal record, "Cohort Default Management Solutions Executive Dashboard: Table of Key Performance Indicators (BPI-HELP-00049480)," August 2010; DeVry internal presentation, "Default Management Update (DEVRY0037185)," August 2010"; Strayer, "Cohort Default Management Solutions Executive Dashboard: Table of Key Performance Indicators (SC-HELP-014911)," July 2010; US Senate HELP Committee, *For Profit Higher Education*, 155.

12. US Senate HELP Committee, *For Profit Higher Education*, figure 1: "General Revenue Corporation's Default Management by Type of Student Relief 2009 and 2010," 156.

13. Ibid.

14. Corinthian, "First Amendment to Cohort Default Management Services Agreement (CCi-00067423)," June 2010; ITT, "First Amendment to Cohort Default Management Services Agreement (ITT-00002281)," June 2010; US Senate HELP Committee, *For Profit Higher Education*, 155.

15. Remington, "RE: RE: Cohort Default Rates—Three Year Calculation Publication (Remington 22-000144)," December 2009; US Senate HELP Committee, *For Profit Higher Education*, 153.

16. US Senate HELP Committee, *For Profit Higher Education*, 156.

17. Corinthian owns more than one-fourth of the schools suspended from the Cal Grant program. Nanette Asimov, "Some For-Profit Colleges Booted from Cal Grants," *San Francisco Chronicle*, February 6, 2012, accessed May

14, 2012, http://www.sfgate.com/cgi-bin/article.cgi?f=/c/a/2012/02/05/BAU11N1V83.DTL; US Senate HELP Committee, *For Profit Higher Education*, 156.

18. Corinthian investor call, "Q3," May 2011; US Senate HELP Committee, *For Profit Higher Education*, 156.

19. Ibid.

20. Corinthian internal presentation, "Financial Aid and Default Prevention Organization (CCi-00057049, at CCi-00057051)," 2010; US Senate HELP Committee, *For Profit Higher Education*, 157.

21. Corinthian internal presentation, "Default Prevention Operations (CCi-00056216)," 2010; US Senate HELP Committee, *For Profit Higher Education*, 157.

22. Corinthian internal presentation, "Counseling at Risk Borrowers (CCi-00056493, at CCi-00056505)," 2010; US Senate Committee, *For Profit Higher Education*, 157.

23. Ibid.

24. Career College Association presentation, "Default Prevention at the Campus Level (HELP-CCA_000001)," June 2009; US Senate HELP Committee, *For Profit Higher Education*, 153.

25. Assuming a 6.8 percent interest rate and 120 monthly payments remaining at the time of forbearance. See "Forbearance Calculator," *Student Loan Finance Corporation*, accessed May 12, 2012, https://www.slfc.com/slfcPresentationTier/slfcPortal.portal?_nfpb=true&planForCollegePortlet_actionOverride=/portlets/tools/CalculateCostOfForb; US Senate HELP Committee, *For Profit Higher Education*, 153.

26. Chancellor University LLC ("Chancellor") is a for-profit higher-education company that enrolled 739 students as of fall 2010 and is based in Seven Hills, OH. US Senate HELP Committee, *For Profit Higher Education*, 153.

27. *Drowning in Debt: Financial Outcomes of Students at For-Profit Colleges, Hearing before the Senate Committee on Health, Education, Labor, and Pensions*, 112th Cong. (2011) (statement of Eric Schmitt, Hampton, IA); US Senate HELP Committee, *For Profit Higher Education*, 153.

28. Supra., 72.

29. Median debt for students receiving a bachelor degree in 2007–2008. *Drowning in Debt: Financial Outcomes of Students at For-Profit Colleges, Hearing Before the Senate Committee on Health, Education, Labor, and Pensions*, 112th Cong. (2011) (statement of Sandy Baum, Policy Analyst, the College Board, and Senior Fellow, George Washington University School of Education and Human Development); US Senate HELP Committee, *For Profit Higher Education*, 113.

30. Ibid.

31. Ibid.

32. Ibid.

33. "Program of Study Information, Program Disclosures," *ITT Technical Institute*, accessed December 14, 2011, http://www.itt-tech.edu/programinfo/psi-ind.pdf; US Senate HELP Committee, *For Profit Higher Education*, 41.

34. "School of Business: Bachelor of Science in Business with a Concentration in Management, Program Disclosures," *University of Phoenix*, accessed December 14, 2011, http://cdn-static.phoenix.edu/content/dam/altcloud/programs/Sealsheets/BSB-M-025B.pdf?cm_sp=Program+Page-_-SealSheet+PDF-_-BSB-M (see program disclosures); "Gainful Employment Disclosures," *DeVry University*, accessed December 14, 2011, http://www.devry.edu/degree-programs/college-business-management/business-administration-consumer-info.jsp; US Senate HELP Committee, *For Profit Higher Education*, 41.

35. "New York State Resident Tuition Plan Rates," *SUNY Buffalo*, 2010, http://studentaccounts.buffalo.edu/tuitionchanges/tuition.php.

36. "Program of Study Information, Program Disclosures," *ITT Technical Institute*, accessed December 14, 2011, http://www.itt-tech.edu/programinfo/psi-ind.pdf; "Program Disclosures," *Everest College*, accessed December 14, 2011, http://disclosures.everest.edu/disclosures/everest-college-ontario- metro.pdf. Everest Colleges and Everest University ("Everest") are brands operated by Corinthian Colleges, Inc. ("Corinthian"), a publicly traded for-profit higher-education company that enrolled 113,818 students in 2010 and is based in Santa Ana, CA. US Senate HELP Committee, *For Profit Higher Education*, 41.

37. "Des Moines Campus Tuition and Fees," *Kaplan*, accessed December 14, 2012, http://desmoines.kaplanuniversity.edu/Pages/tuition.aspx; "School of Business: Bachelor of Science in Business with a Concentration in Management, Program Disclosures," *University of Phoenix*, accessed December 14, 2011, http://cdnstatic.phoenix.edu/content/dam/altcloud/programs/Sealsheets/BSB-M-025B.pdf?cm_sp=Program+Page-_-SealSheet+PDF-_-BSB-M (see program disclosures); US Senate HELP Committee, *For Profit Higher Education*, 41.

38. CollegeBoard Advocacy and Policy Center, "Trends in College Pricing 2011," *College Board*, 2011, accessed May 3, 2012, http://trends.collegeboard.org/downloads/College_Pricing_2011.pdf, 10 ; US Senate HELP Committee, *For Profit Higher Education*, 41.

39. Lincoln external e-mail, "re: BBB Complaint Case#42006975(Ref # 58-6023-42006975-4-12200) (LINC0000001, at LINC0000003)," January 2007. The Better Business Bureau did not pursue an investigation of this complaint. US Senate HELP Committee, *For Profit Higher Education*, 113.

40. ITT external correspondence, "re: ITT Technical Institute (ITT-00009376, at ITT-00009383)" (response to student's complaint with text of student's complaint enclosed), January 2009; US Senate HELP Committee, *For Profit Higher Education*, 113.

41. ITT external correspondence, "Notice of Student Complaint to Better Business Bureau (ITT-00009785, at ITT-00009786)," July 2010; US Senate HELP Committee, *For Profit Higher Education*, 113.

42. "Information for Financial Aid Professionals, Cohort Default Rates Charts," *US Department of Education*, 2010, accessed May 3, 2012, http://ifap.ed.gov/eannouncements/attachments/122010CDRlifetimerateattach-ment2ratechart2010.pdf; US Senate HELP Committee, *For Profit Higher Education*, 116.

43. US Senate HELP Committee, *For Profit Higher Education*, figure: "Staffing Levels at 24 For-Profit Education Companies 2007–10," 95. This indicates annual student enrollment as well as staffing levels.

8. CONGRESSIONAL CONSPIRACY

1. United States Senate Health, Education, Labor, and Pensions Committee (US Senate HELP Committee), *For Profit Higher Education: The Failure to Safeguard the Federal Investment and Ensure Student Success*, Majority Committee Staff Report and Accompanying Minority Committee Staff Views, July 30, 2012, figure 1, "Profit Margins (Operating Income) at For-Profit Education Companies in 2009," 83.

2. Apollo Group, Inc., "Form 10-K for period ending 8/31/2009"; US Senate HELP Committee, *For Profit Higher Education*, 83.

3. "Title IV Program Volume Report for Apollo," *US Department of Education, Federal Student Aid Data Center*, 2012. http://federalstuden-taid.ed.gov/datacenter/programmatic.html; US Senate HELP Committee, *For Profit Higher Education*, 83.

4. Ibid.

5. Supra., 91.

6. US Senate HELP Committee, *For Profit Higher Education*, figure 1, "Five Highest Paid Executives at Publicly Traded For-Profit Education Companies in 2009," 84.

7. Ibid.

8. Supra., 92.

9. "Salaries of Private-College Presidents," *Chronicle of Higher Education*, 2009, accessed May 24, 2012, http://chronicle.com/article/Sortable-Table-Sala-

ries-of/129982; US Senate HELP Committee, *For Profit Higher Education*, 84.

10. *Drowning in Debt: Financial Outcomes of Students at For-Profit Colleges Hearing before the Senate Committee on Health, Education, Labor, and Pensions*, 112th Cong. (2011) (statement of Sandy Baum, Policy Analyst, the College Board, and Senior Fellow, George Washington University School of Education and Human Development); US Senate HELP Committee, *For Profit Higher Education*, 84.

11. US Senate HELP Committee, *For Profit Higher Education*, appendix 17, "Highest Paid Executives by Sector, A17-6." Football coaches at some nonprofit and public schools are paid more than the college president. The top five salaries for coaches in 2011 are University of Texas with $5.1 million, University of Alabama with $4.8 million, University of Oklahoma with $4 million, Louisiana State University with $3.8 million, and University of Iowa with $3.7 million. See Christopher Schnaars, Jodi Upton, and Kristin DeRamus, "College Football Coach Salary Database," *USA Today* Accessed May 20, 2012, http://www.usatoday.com/sports/college/football/story/2011-11-17/cover-college-football-coaches-salaries-rise/51242232/1. Sandy Baum, policy analyst at the College Board and senior fellow at George Washington University School of Education and Human Development, noted the mismatch in her testimony before the committee: "Average compensation for the five highest-paid public university chief executives in 2009–10 was $860,000. The five highest-paid Ivy League presidents received an average of $1.3 million in 2008–09. The top five leaders of publicly traded for-profit postsecondary institutions received an average of $10.5 million in 2009." *Drowning in Debt* (Baum).

12. US Senate HELP Committee, *For Profit Higher Education*, 83.

13. *For-Profit Colleges: Undercover Testing Finds Colleges Encouraged Fraud and Engaged in Deceptive and Questionable Marketing Practices Hearing before the Senate Committee on Health, Education, Labor, and Pensions*, 111th Cong. (August 4, 2010) (statement of Gregory D. Kuntz, Managing Director Forensics Audits and Special Investigations), 1.

14. Nick Anderson, "For-Profit Schools Lobby to Avoid Proposed Federal Aid Rule," *Washington Post*, October 22, 2010, accessed June 24, 2013, http://www.washingtonpost.com/wp-dyn/content/article/2010/10/22/AR2010102200093.html.

15. President Barack Obama (speech, University of Texas, August 9, 2010), accessed June 2, 2013, http://www.kxan.com/dpp/news/politics/transcript-president-obamas-speech.

16. US Senate HELP Committee, *For Profit Higher Education*, 85.

17. Eric Lichtblau, "With Lobbying Blitz, For-Profit Colleges Diluted New Rules," *New York Times*, December 9, 2011, accessed May 3, 2012, http://

www.nytimes.com/2011/12/10/us/politics/for-profit-college-rules-scaled-back-after-lobbying.html?pagewanted=all; US Senate HELP Committee, *For Profit Higher Education*, 86.

18. Ibid.

19. Ibid.

20. Michael Kellermann and Kenneth A. Shepsle, "Congressional Careers, Committee Assignments, and Seniority Randomization in the U.S. House of Representatives," *Quarterly Journal of Political Science* (August 14, 2007), accessed July 10, 2013, www.wcfia.harvard.edu/sites/default/files/Shepsle_Congressional.pdf, 2.

21. Gary Cox and Matthew McCubbins, *Legislative Leviathan: Party Government in the House* (Berkeley: University of California Press, 1993), 186.

22. Jon Bond and Kevin Smith, *The Promise and Performance of American Democracy* (Boston: Cengage Learning, 2010), 438.

23. Ibid.

24. "Stage 3: The Bill Goes to Committee," *LexisNexis*, 2007, accessed July 10, 2013, http://www.lexisnexis.com/help/cu/the_legislative_process/Stage_3.htm.

25. Ibid.

26. Ibid.

27. Donny Shaw, "Only Four Percent of Bills Become Law, Sunlight Foundation," *Huffington Post*, August, 25, 2009, accessed July 10, 2013, http://www.huffingtonpost.com/wires/2009/08/25/the-vast-majority-of-bill_ws_268630.html.

28. "House Committee on Education and the Workforce," *GovTrack*, accessed July 10, 2013, http://www.govtrack.us/congress/committees/HSED.

29. "John Kline: Top 20 Contributors, 2007–2008," *Center for Responsive Politics*, accessed July 12, 2013, http://www.opensecrets.org/politicians/contrib.php?cycle=2008&cid=N00004436&type=I.

30. "Rep. John Kline: Top Industries, 2011–2012," *Center for Responsive Politics*, accessed July 12, 2013, http://www.opensecrets.org/politicians/industries.php?cycle=2012&cid=N00004436&type=I.

31. "John Kline: Top 20 Contributors, 2011–2012," *Center for Responsive Politics*, accessed July 12, 2013, http://www.opensecrets.org/politicians/contrib.php?cycle=2012&cid=N00004436&type=I.

32. Ibid.

33. Ibid.

34. Ibid.

35. "House Committee on Education and the Workforce: Subcommittees," *GovTrack*, accessed July 12, 2013, http://www.govtrack.us/congress/committees/HSED#subcommittees.

36. "House Committee on Education and the Workforce: House Subcommittee on Higher Education and Workforce Training," *GovTrack*, accessed July 12, 2013, http://www.govtrack.us/congress/committees/HSED/13.

37. "Rep. Virginia Foxx: Top Industries, 2011–2012," *Center for Responsive Politics*, accessed July 12, 2013, http://www.opensecrets.org/politicians/industries.php?cycle=2012&cid=N00026166&type=I&newmem=N.

38. "Virginia Foxx: Top 20 Contributors, 2011–2012," *Center for Responsive Politics*, accessed July 12, 2013, http://www.opensecrets.org/politicians/contrib.php?cycle=2012&cid=N00026166&type=I.

39. Ibid.

40. Supra., 97.

41. "Buck McKeon: Career Profile (since 1989): Top Contributors," *Center for Responsive Politics*, accessed July 12, 2013, http://www.opensecrets.org/politicians/contrib.php?cycle=Career&type=I&cid=N00006882&newMem=N&recs=20.

42. "Rules of the Committee on Education and the Workforce, US House of Representative: 113th Congress, Adopted January 22, 2013," Accessed July 13, 2012, www.gpo.gov/fdsys/pkg/CPRT-113HPRT78267/html/CPRT-113HPRT78267.htm, 8.

43. "Influence and Lobbying," *Center for Responsive Politics*, accessed July 12, 2013, http://www.opensecrets.org/influence.

44. "Text of the College Student Rebate Act of 2012," *GovTrack*, September 13, 2012, accessed July 12, 2013, http://www.govtrack.us/congress/bills/112/hr6407/text.

45. Ibid.

46. "Text of the Protecting Financial Aid for Students and Taxpayers Act," *GovTrack*, January 22, 2013, accessed July 12, 2013, http://www.govtrack.us/congress/bills/113/hr340/text.

9. ERADICATION

1. John D. Rockefeller Jr., 1874–1960, Rockefeller Archive Center. On July 8, 1941, in a radio broadcast appeal on behalf of the USO and the National War Fund, he gave this statement of principles that was widely reprinted under the title, "I Believe." These principles were first penned by his father and eventually publicly revealed in this address.

2. United States Senate Health, Education, Labor, and Pensions Committee (US Senate HELP Committee), *For Profit Higher Education: The Failure to Safeguard the Federal Investment and Ensure Student Success*, Majority

Committee Staff Report and Accompanying Minority Committee Staff Views, July 30, 2012, "Recommendations," 171–73.

3. "34 CFR 668.187: Consequences of Cohort Default Rates on Your Ability to Participate in Title IV, HEA Programs," *Legal Information Institute, Cornell University Law School*, accessed March 30, 2014, http://www.law.cornell.edu/cfr/text/34/668.187.

4. Higher Education Act of 1965, Chapter VI: Office of Postsecondary Education, Higher Education, 34 CFR Ch. VI (7–1–12 Edition) §668.1(a): Subpart A—General: Scope, 461, *US Government Printing Office*, accessed July 17, 2013, http://www.gpo.gov/fdsys/search/pagede-tails.action?collectionCode=CFR&search-Path=Title+34%2FSubtitle+B%2FChapter+Vi%2FPart+668&granu-leId=CFR-2012-title34-vol3-sec600-5&packageId=CFR-2012-title34-vol3&old-Path=Title+34%2FSubtitle+B%2FChapter+Vi%2FPart+600%2FSubpart+A&fromPageDetails=true&collapse=true&ycord=1984.

5. Higher Education Act of 1965, Chapter VI: Office of Postsecondary Education, Higher Education, 34 CFR Ch. VI (7–1–12 Edition) §600.4(a): Institution of higher education, *US Government Printing Office*, accessed July 17, 2013, http://www.gpo.gov/fdsys/search/pagede-tails.action?collectionCode=CFR&search-Path=Title+34%2FSubtitle+B%2FChapter+Vi%2FPart+668&granu-leId=CFR-2012-title34-vol3-sec600-5&packageId=CFR-2012-title34-vol3&old-Path=Title+34%2FSubtitle+B%2FChapter+Vi%2FPart+600%2FSubpart+A&fromPageDetails=true&collapse=true&ycord=1984.

6. Higher Education Act of 1965, Chapter VI: Office of Postsecondary Education, Higher Education, 34 CFR Ch. VI (7–1–12 Edition) §600.5(a): Proprietary institution of higher education, *US Government Printing Office*, accessed July 17, 2013, http://www.gpo.gov/fdsys/search/pagede-tails.action?collectionCode=CFR&search-Path=Title+34%2FSubtitle+B%2FChapter+Vi%2FPart+668&granu-leId=CFR-2012-title34-vol3-sec600-5&packageId=CFR-2012-title34-vol3&old-Path=Title+34%2FSubtitle+B%2FChapter+Vi%2FPart+600%2FSubpart+A&fromPageDetails=true&collapse=true&ycord=1984.

7. Higher Education Act of 1965, Chapter VI: Office of Postsecondary Education, Higher Education, 34 CFR Ch. VI (7–1–12 Edition) §600.7: Conditions of institutional ineligibility, *US Government Printing Office*, accessed July 17, 2013, http://www.gpo.gov/fdsys/search/pagede-tails.action?collectionCode=CFR&search-

Path=Title+34%2FSubtitle+B%2FChapter+Vi%2FPart+668&granu-
leId=CFR-2012-title34-vol3-sec600-5&packageId=CFR-2012-title34-vol3&
old-
Path=Title+34%2FSubtitle+B%2FChapter+Vi%2FPart+600%2FSubpart+A
&fromPageDetails=true&collapse=true&ycord=1984.

   8. Ibid., § 600.7 (3)(ii).

   9. Mark Greenblatt, "Whistle-Blower: For-Profit College Operator Allegedly Inflates Job Placement Rates," *ABC News*, November 26, 2012, accessed
July 18, 2013, http://abcnews.go.com/US/whistle-blower-profit-college-opera-
tor-allegedly-inflates-job/story?id=17810902.

   10. US Senate HELP Committee, *For Profit Higher Education*, "Summary
of Selected For-Profit Education Company Placement Investigations," 164.

   11. Blake Ellis, "U.S. to Corinthian Colleges: Forgive $500 Million in Stu-
dent Loans," *CNN Money*, September 16, 2014, http://money.cnn.com/2014/
09/16/pf/college/cfpb-corinthian-lawsuit.

   12. Kevin Connell, "Leveling the Corinthian Leviathan," *Tangents USA*,
June 9, 2015, https://tangentsusa.wordpress.com/2015/06/09/leveling-the-co-
rinthian.

   13. On April 27, 2015, Corinthian Colleges, Inc., announced that it had
terminated all operations and discontinued instruction at its remaining twenty-
eight ground campuses. Locations that had been closed span from Corinthian's
thirteen remaining Everest and WyoTech campuses in California to the Everest College Phoenix and Everest Online Tempe in Arizona as well as the
Everest Institute in New York and the 150-year-old Heald College, which
housed ten locations in California, one in Hawaii, and one in Oregon.

   14. Kevin Connell, "Leveling the Corinthian Leviathan," 2015.

   15. Ibid.

   16. Emily Hanford, "The Story of the University of Phoenix," *American
Public Media*, accessed July 18, 2013, http://americanradiow-
orks.publicradio.org/features/tomorrows-college/phoenix/story-of-university-
of-phoenix.html.

   17. Ibid.

   18. Alexander Hamilton, "Federalist Paper 21, December 12, 1787," in *The
Federalist: Alexander Hamilton, James Madison, and John Jay*, introduction
and notes by Robert A. Ferguson (New York: Barnes and Noble, 2005), 111.

   19. "Articles of Confederation: Article I, July 9, 1778," in *The Essential
Federalist and Anti-Federalist Papers*, by David Wooten (Indianapolis: Hackett, 2003).

   20. "The United States Constitution: Preamble, September 17, 1787," in
The Essential Federalist and Anti-Federalist Papers, by David Wooten (Indianapolis: Hackett, 2003).

21. "The United States Constitution: Bill of Rights (Adopted as Amending the Constitution, December 15, 1791)," in *The Essential Federalist and Anti-Federalist Papers*, by David Wooten (Indianapolis: Hackett, 2003).

22. James Madison, "Federalist 39, January 16, 1788," in *The Essential Federalist and Anti-Federalist Papers*, by David Wooten (Indianapolis: Hackett, 2003).

23. Ibid.

24. Ibid.

25. Ibid.

26. Ibid.

27. "The United States Constitution: Article I, Section 8, September 17, 1787," in *The Essential Federalist and Anti-Federalist Papers*, by David Wooten (Indianapolis: Hackett, 2003).

28. "*McCulloch v. Maryland*," Oyez, IIT Chicago-Kent College of Law, accessed August 20, 2013, http://www.oyez.org/cases/1792-1850/1819/1819_0.

29. "Alexander Hamilton, Report on Manufactures," in *The Founders' Constitution*, December 5, 1791, accessed August 21, 2013, http://press-pubs.uchicago.edu/founders/documents/v1ch4s31.html.

30. Douglas A. Irwin, "The Aftermath of Hamilton's 'Report on Manufacture,'" *Journal of Economic History* 64 (September 2004), Accessed August 21, 2013, http://www.nber.org/papers/w9943.

31. "*Gibbons v. Ogden*," Oyez, IIT Chicago-Kent College of Law, accessed August 21, 2013, http://www.oyez.org/cases/1792-1850/1824/1824_0. "The Court found that New York's licensing requirement for out-of-state operators was inconsistent with a congressional act regulating the coasting trade. The New York law was invalid by virtue of the Supremacy Clause. In his opinion, Chief Justice Marshall developed a clear definition of the word commerce, which included navigation on interstate waterways. He also gave meaning to the phrase 'among the several states' in the Commerce Clause. Marshall's was one of the earliest and most influential opinions concerning this important clause. He concluded that regulation of navigation by steamboat operators and others for purposes of conducting interstate commerce was a power reserved to and exercised by the Congress."

32. "James Madison to Andrew Stevenson," *The Founder's Constitution*, November 27, 1830, accessed August 21, 2013, http://press-pubs.uchicago.edu/founders/documents/a1_8_1s27.html.

33. Alexander Hamilton, "Federalist Paper 22, December 14, 1787," in *The Federalist: Alexander Hamilton, James Madison, and John Jay*, introduction and notes by Robert A. Ferguson (New York: Barnes and Noble, 2005), 111.

34. "*New York v. United States* (91-543), 488 U.S. 1041 (1992)," *LLI, Cornell University Law School*, accessed August 22, 2013, http://

www.law.cornell.edu/supct/html/91-543.ZO.html. In *New York v. United States*, the court found that the "Take Title" provision of the Low-Level Radioactive Waste Policy Amendments Act of 1985 exceeded Congress's power under the Commerce Clause.

35. *"Printz v. United States* (95-1478), 521 U.S. 898 (1997)," *LLI, Cornell University Law School*, accessed August 22, 2013, http://www.law.cornell.edu/supct/html/95-1478.ZO.html. Under *Printz v. United States*, the court ruled certain interim provisions of the Brady Handgun Violence Prevention Act to be unconstitutional. Unlike *New York v. United States*, which concerned federal mandates targeting state legislatures, this case concerned provisions that directed local law enforcement officers (executive branch officials) to monitor gun purchases under the specific guidelines of the interim provisions of the Brady Act, a federal mandate.

36. *"United States v. Butler,"* *LLI, Cornell University Law School*, accessed August 22, 2013, http://www.law.cornell.edu/supct/html/historics/USSC_CR_0297_0001_ZS.html.

37. Ibid.

38. Ibid.

39. Ibid., at 66.

40. *"Steward Machine Company v. Davis,"* *Oyez, IIT Chicago-Kent College of Law*, accessed August 22, 2013, http://today.oyez.org/cases/1901-1939/1936/1936_837.

41. Ibid.

42. *"South Dakota v. Dole,"* *Oyez, IIT Chicago-Kent College of Law*, accessed August 10, 2013, http://www.oyez.org/cases/1980-1989/1986/1986_86_260#sort=ideology.

43. Ibid.

44. Ibid.

45. Ibid.

46. Erwin Chemerinsky, "Protecting the Spending Power," *Chapman Law Review* 4 (2001), 104; *"South Dakota v. Dole."*

47. Ibid.

48. Jim C., 235 F.3d at 1082, in Chemerinsky, "Protecting the Spending Power," 105; *"South Dakota v. Dole."*

49. *"Steward Machine Company v. Davis,"* at 589–90; Chemerinsky, "Protecting the Spending Power," 105; *"South Dakota v. Dole."*

50. "Opinion of Roberts, C. J.," *National Federation of Independent Business v. Sebelius*, 567 U.S. (2012), accessed November 12, 2013, http://www.supremecourt.gov/opinions/11pdf/11-393c3a2.pdf, 47.

51. "Opinion of Ginsburg, J.," *National Federation of Independent Business v. Sebelius*, 567 U.S. (2012), accessed November 12, 2013,http://www.supremecourt.gov/opinions/11pdf/11-393c3a2.pdf, 39.

52. Ibid.

53. "Opinion of Roberts," 48–49.

54. Ibid., 51, 54.

55. Ibid., 52.

56. "Opinion of Ginsburg," 45.

57. Ibid., 46, 47.

58. "Scalia, Kennedy, Thomas, and Alito, J.J., Dissenting," *National Federation of Independent Business v. Sebelius*, 567 U.S. (2012), accessed November 12, 2013, http://www.supremecourt.gov/opinions/11pdf/11-393c3a2.pdf, 32.

59. Ibid., 31.

60. "Opinion of Roberts," 47.

61. Supra., 94.

62. Stephen Q. Cornman, "Revenues and Expenditures for Public Elementary and Secondary School Districts: School Year 2009–10 (Fiscal Year 2010)," *National Center for Education Statistics, US Department of Education*, April 2013, accessed September 1, 2013, http://nces.ed.gov/pubs2013/2013307.pdf.

10. DIPLOMAS FOR JOBS, NOT PINK SLIPS

1. Stephen Q. Cornman, "Revenues and Expenditures for Public Elementary and Secondary School Districts: School Year 2009–10 (Fiscal Year 2010)," *National Center for Education Statistics*, April 2013, http://nces.ed.gov/pubs2013/2013307.pdf.

2. Ibid.

3. Ibid.

4. Ibid.

5. Ibid.

6. Benjamin Herold, "Philadelphia School Closures: 37 Targeted, Dozens More to Relocate or Reconfigure," *Huffington Post: Education*, December 13, 2012, accessed September 1, 2013, http://www.huffingtonpost.com/2012/12/13/philadelphia-school-closu_n_2295660.html.

7. Ibid.

8. Erica Williams, Michael Leachman, and Nicholas Johnson, "State Budget Cuts in the New Fiscal Year Are Unnecessarily Harmful: Cuts Are Hitting Hard at Education, Health Care, and State Economies," *Center on Budget and Policy Priorities*, July 28, 2011, accessed September 1, 2013, http://www.cbpp.org/cms/?fa=view&id=3550.

9. Ibid.

10. Ibid.

11. Barack Obama, "Excerpts of the President's Remarks in Warren, Michigan and Fact Sheet on the American Graduation Initiative," *The White House, Office of the Press Secretary*, July 14, 2009, accessed September 18, 2013, http://www.whitehouse.gov/the_press_office/Excerpts-of-the-Presidents-remarks-in-Warren-Michigan-and-fact-sheet-on-the-American-Graduation-Initiative.

12. Ibid.

13. Ibid.

14. "Table 6. Occupations with the most job growth, 2014–24," *United States Department of Labor, Bureau of Labor Statistics*, accessed September 18, 2013, http://www.bls.gov/news.release/ecopro.t06.htm.

15. "Table 8. Occupations with the largest projected number of job openings due to growth and replacement needs, 2012 and projected 2022," *United States Department of Labor: Bureau of Labor Statistics*, accessed September 18, 2013, http://www.bls.gov/news.release/ecopro.t08.htm.

16. "Occupational Employment Statistics: May 2012 Metropolitan and Nonmetropolitan Area Occupational Employment and Wage Estimates" *United States Department of Labor, Bureau of Labor Statistics*, accessed September 18, 2013, http://www.bls.gov/oes/current/oes_40380.htm.

17. Ibid.

18. Obama, "Excerpts."

19. "S. 1269 (113th): Community College to Career Fund Act," *GovTrack*, July 8, 2013, accessed September 18, 2013, http://www.govtrack.us/congress/bills/113/s1269.

20. Obama, "Excerpts."

21. Ibid.

22. "Complete College Georgia: Georgia's Higher Education Completion Plan 2012," *University System of Georgia*, November 2011, accessed September 18, 2013, http://www.usg.edu/educational_access/documents/GaHigherEducationCompletionPlan2012.pdf.

23. Rob Jenkins, "Online Classes and College Completion," *Chronicle of Higher Education*, March 13, 2012, accessed September 18, 2013, http://chronicle.com/article/article-content/131133.

24. "Evaluation of Evidence-Based Practices in Online Learning: A Meta-Analysis and Review of Online Learning Studies," *Educause*, June 26, 2009, accessed September 18, 2013, http://www.educause.edu/library/resources/evaluation-evidence-based-practices-online-learning-meta-analysis-and-review-online-learning-studies.

25. Jenkins, "Online Classes."

26. Ibid.
27. Ibid.
28. Ibid.
29. Ibid.
30. Ibid.
31. Douglas A. Guiffrida, Martin F. Lynch, Andrew F. Wall, and Darlene S. Abel, "Do Reasons for Attending College Affect Academic Outcomes? A Test of a Motivational Model from a Self-Determination Theory Perspective," *Journal of College Student Development* 54, no.2 (March/April 2013), 121–39.
32. Ibid., 129.
33. United States Senate Health, Education, Labor, and Pensions Committee (US Senate HELP Committee), *For Profit Higher Education: The Failure to Safeguard the Federal Investment and Ensure Student Success*, Majority Committee Staff Report and Accompanying Minority Committee Staff Views, July 30, 2012, table: "Retention Rates for Online and Campus Students in 2010," 76.

ABOUT THE AUTHOR

Kevin Connell is a native of Rochester, New York, where he earned a B.A. in political science from the University of Rochester. After graduating cum laude and Phi Beta Kappa from the University of Rochester, Kevin now attends William & Mary Law School, where he is expected to graduate in 2018 with the intent to practice law and enter politics.

41087053R00104

Made in the USA
Middletown, DE
03 March 2017